Confederate Cavalrymen of the Civil War

Philip Katcher • Illustrated by Gerry Embleton

This American edition first published in 2003 by Raintree, a division of Reed Elsevier Inc., Chicago, Illinois, by arrangement with Osprey Publishing Limited, Oxford, England.

For information, address the publisher:
Raintree, 100 N. LaSalle, Suite 1200, Chicago, IL 60602

First published 2002
Under the title *Warrior 54: Confederate Cavalryman 1861–1865*
By Osprey Publishing Limited, Elms Court, Chapel Way, Botley, Oxford, OX2 9LP
© 2002 Osprey Publishing Limited
All rights reserved.

ISBN 1-4109-0114-9

03 04 05 06 07   10 9 8 7 6 5 4 3 2 1

Library of Congress Cataloging-in-Publication Data

Katcher, Philip R. N.
  [Confederate cavalryman, 1861-65]
  Confederate cavalrymen of the Civil War / Philip Katcher.
    v. cm. -- (A soldier's life)
Originally published: Confederate cavalryman, 1861-65. Oxford [England] : Osprey, 2002, in series: Warrior.
Includes bibliographical references and index.
Contents: Regular cavalry -- Recruiting -- Training, uniforms, equipment, and weapons -- Everyday life -- Campaign life -- Battle -- Partisan rangers -- Scouts and couriers.
  ISBN 1-4109-0114-9 (lib. bdg.)
  1. Confederate States of America. Army. Cavalry--History--Juvenile literature. 2. Soldiers--Confederate States of America--History--Juvenile literature. 3. United States--History--Civil War, 1861-1865--Cavalry operations--Juvenile literature. [1. Confederate States of America. Army. Cavalry--History. 2. Soldiers--Confederate States of America--History. 3. United States--History--Civil War, 1861-1865--Cavalry operations.] I. Title. II. Series.
  E546.5.K38 2003
  973.7'42--dc21
                    2003005280

Author: Philip Katcher
Illustrator: Gerry Embleton
Editor: Thomas Lowres
Design: Ken Vail Graphic Design, Cambridge, UK
Index by Alan Rutter
Originated by Magnet Harlequin, Uxbridge, UK
Printed in China through World Print Ltd.

Artist's note

Readers may care to note that the original paintings from which the color plates in this book were prepared are available for private sale. All reproduction copyright whatsoever is retained by the Publishers. All enquiries should be addressed to:

Scorpio Gallery
PO Box 475
Hailsham
E Sussex
BN27 2SL

Acknowledgments

All illustrations are author's own collection unless otherwise indicated.

CONTENTS

CONFEDERATE CAVALRYMEN OF THE CIVIL WAR

INTRODUCTION

"The Confederacy had from the beginning attached greater importance to the cavalry arm of the service than had the North," recalled Private Luther Hopkins, 6th Virginia Cavalry, after the war, "and many had been the daring raids that [Army of Northern Virginia cavalry commander J.E.B.] Stuart made within the enemy's lines, capturing thousands of wagons laden with military stores, and many thousand prisoners."

The average Southerner of the mid-19th century had been bred to ride horses. The society from which he came was largely rural, with poor roads and a lack of available public transportation. Men rode horseback wherever they went. Added to this, the Southerner of the period had a long history of using firearms, either for hunting for food or simply for sport.

Mounted Texans form new cavalry units in front of the shrine of the Texas fight for independence against Mexico, the Alamo, in San Antonio, in 1861. (*Military Images* magazine)

It is also significant that a large percentage of the Southern officers who resigned their U.S. Army commissions were cavalrymen. In fact, Robert E. Lee and Albert Sidney Johnston both came from the 2nd U.S. Cavalry just before the war. As a result, Confederate cavalry was, somewhat inevitably, considered far superior to that of the Union.

Cavalry became even more popular as the war progressed, since duty there was perceived as easier than in any other branch of service. One infantryman wrote home advising that his younger brother should "by all means to join the Cavalry—and bear in mind that a private in the Infantry is the worse place he can possible be put into in this war—so if he wants to have a good time join the Cavalry."

Confederate cavalry was a unique branch of service. It was "...divided into four quite distinct classes, the functions of which differed completely," explained German professional soldier Captain Justus Scheibert, a visitor to the Confederacy in 1863. Scheibert continued:

> 1. *Regular Cavalry.* Combined into regiments, brigades, and divisions for skirmishes, battles, and raids in force. Stuart's, Van Dorn's, and Morgan's cavalry belong to this group. 2. *Partisan Rangers.* A kind of free corps that was not limited with respect to numbers. Their raids under a well-known commander (Mosby is

the most famous one) are the most adventurous and the most stirring events of recent times. Their pay was their booty, which they were required to sell to the War Department at a fair price. 3. *Scouts.* Drawn mostly from the Indian states of the West, they acted on their own responsibility. They had to be in enemy territory from time to time and to report on all movements of the enemy. They usually rode through the outposts at night and hid in the daytime in dense thickets or in houses occupied by Southern sympathizers. They always had to be in uniform, and they differed from spies in this respect. 4. *Couriers.* Young, skilled, nimble horsemen on excellent mounts performed orderly service and were attached to headquarters, so that the commanding general had sixty [men], a corps twelve, a division six, and a brigade three, each ready for duty.

Captain William McDonald, ordinance officer of the Army of Northern Virginia's Laurel Brigade of cavalry pointed out in his brigade history that, when seen in review, there were real distinctions among the different regiments. "Each regiment appeared different from each other, and in turn evinced some peculiarity that evoked admiration from the lookers-on," wrote McDonald:

The Carolinians were easily distinguished. They rode with military primness and were mounted on steeds of delicately-shaped limbs with glistening eyes and full of fire and motion. At their head rode Wade Hampton, then in the full bloom of manhood and looking every inch the soldier he proved himself to be. The Lower Virginians challenged attention by the graceful nonchalance of their riding, and the easy with which they moved along, yet having the steady front of veterans. The Valley and Piedmont men, of which Jones' brigade was composed, were from the blue-grass section, and the strong, well-limbed horses gave to their squadrons an impression of massive and warlike strength. The riders like centaurs appeared almost one with their steeds. General [William E.] Jones rode at their head, evidently proud of his command, but with disdainful air, for he hated the "pomp and circumstance of war."

Not all cavalrymen were expert soldiers. Private Hopkins, 6th Virginia Cavalry recalled:

Within every regiment there is a Company Q. Company Q is composed of lame ducks, cowards, shirkers, dead-beats, generally, and also a large sprinkling of good soldiers, who, for some reason or another, are not fit for duty. Sometimes this company is quite large. It depends upon the weather, the

This sketch "by one of our most reliable artists" of a Texas Ranger appeared in *Harper's Weekly* on July 6, 1862. The caption read, "Ben McCullough's Texan Rangers are described as a desperate set of fellows. They number one thousand half savages, each of whom is mounted upon a mustang horse. Each is armed with a pair of Colt's Navy revolvers, a rifle, a tomahawk, a Texas Bowieknife, and a lasso. They are described as being very dexterous in the use of the latter." (*Military Images* magazine)

closeness of the enemy, and the duties that are being exacted. Bad weather will drive in all rheumatics; the coming battle will drive in the cowards; hard marching and picket duty will bring in the lazy. But then, as I have just said, there were some good soldiers among them – the slightly wounded or those suffering from any disability.

REGULAR CAVALRY

Recruiting

At the outset of war in 1861 the Confederate government immediately authorized an army that included cavalry as one of the three combat branches of service. A handful of volunteer militia cavalry companies swiftly volunteered as units. Most of these were made up of wealthy, socially prominent members. The Georgia Hussars, from Savannah, Georgia, for example, had an initial outfit that cost $25,000, according to one of its members, Captain Alexander Duncan.

However, there were not enough militia cavalry companies to fill the total need. Local civic leaders began organizing new companies and regiments right away. Unlike the cavalry from any other civilized nation though, these men would have to provide their own horses, as neither central nor state governments had the ability to do so for them. Initially, men also had to supply their own weapons, clothing, and equipment. Each recruit was credited with the value of the horse and equipment he brought. For example, within the 4th Texas Cavalry, one private was credited with a black gelding worth $100, a rawhide skeleton saddle worth $25, saddlebags worth $4, two blankets worth $7, a bridle worth $2, a double-barreled shotgun worth $25, underclothing worth $8, coat and trousers worth $16, a pair of boots worth $6, and a canteen, cup, knife, and belt worth $3. The private had come with a total of $196 worth of equipment from home. His horse was better than usual, as the 1861 tax rolls in his home county records that the average horse was worth only $40.

Although eventually the central Confederate government was to take over issuing all other items, horses had to be provided by the men themselves throughout the war. Consequently, as the war progressed, men had to be allowed to return home when their horses were either killed in action or died from disease to try to buy a new one. Texas officials solved this problem by rounding up wild mustangs, bringing them in herds to where prospective cavalrymen could pick out one to buy and train. Generally, however, as a result of the personal owner requirements, most Confederate cavalry units were always understrength.

The policy of cavalrymen providing their own horses was not universally approved of by generals in

Private J.T. Hawkins, 5th Kentucky Cavalry, wears typical underclothes, including a white shirt (which would become rare as the war dragged on), and civilian boots and trousers. The broad-brimmed hat was the preferred headgear of the cavalry. This was the usual dress for recruits. (John Sickles collection)

the field. "If the Government would furnish horses to cavalry enlisted for three years, or during the war, I think I could raise a battalion very rapidly of the best material. Men cannot buy their horses and equipments. That day has gone by," wrote Brigadier-General H. Marshall to Richmond on March 13, 1862. "If I had the control I never would mount a volunteer upon his own horse or have in cavalry service any animal but a public one. A long experience as a cavalry officer with volunteers has made this one of my fixed opinions."

Indeed, Captain Charles Blackford, 2nd Virginia Cavalry wrote home in late 1862:

> My company is becoming smaller and smaller through sickness, wounds and lack of horses, chiefly the latter. It is, as you well know, difficult for a city company like ours to keep up in mounts. My men do not have farms, or relatives and neighbors with farms from whom they can draw when their horses get killed or disabled, but have to purchase their horses at prices even I hesitate to pay. I believe this is the only army in history where the men have to furnish their own horses and it is the main weakness of our cavalry. To me to lose a horse is to lose a man, as they cannot afford a remount and new recruits with horses of their own are almost nil.

Private William Campbell, Co. D, 2nd Kentucky Cavalry, wears a typical version of the waist-length jacket, which was preferred for mounted use. (John Sickles collection)

The horse replacement problem was never properly solved. In fact, John Casler, 11th Virginia Cavalry, reported that his "brigade was disbanded for the winter, and sent to different portions of the country to get provisions for their horses."

The men themselves remained eager to join the cavalry, even if they needed their own horses. They felt that they were defending their homes against Northern aggression and needed no great sums of money (which was good, since they often went unpaid for long periods of time) or harsh discipline to fight. Moreover, they generally joined local units in which they knew most other members, and they were further motivated to fight well just to keep face, or to "maintain their honor," as they would have said.

Captain William McDonald, ordnance officer of the Army of Northern Virginia's Laurel Brigade of cavalry, noted that recruiting was easy since, "This service was exacting but attractive on account of its comparative freedom from restraint, and the opportunities it afforded for personal adventure." Indeed, in the west virtually nobody walked, due to the long distances between destinations, and infantry units were hard to recruit, while cavalry units filled up quickly.

Texas, for example, raised 2.4 cavalry units for every one infantry unit raised. In the Trans-Mississippi Department alone, Texas organized 39 mounted regiments and another ten separate battalions. "The people of Texas live on horseback," the state's governor explained to the central government in Richmond, "and it is with great aversion they enlist in the infantry. Cavalry, efficient cavalry, can be obtained from this State almost to the extent of the male population, but infantry is difficult to furnish."

The average strength in each Texas cavalry regiment was 947 officers and men, with 440 officers and men in each battalion. "At the outbreak of the war it was found very difficult to raise infantry in Texas," observed visiting English officer Arthur Fremantle, "as no Texan walks a yard if he can help it. Many mounted regiments were therefore organized and afterwards dismounted."

The make-up of cavalry units was, like the South itself, basically agrarian. In, for example, the 1st Texas Cavalry just over half (55 percent) came from farming or stock raising backgrounds. Another 11 percent were professionals, such as store clerks and mechanics, while eight percent were skilled laborers, and five percent were unskilled laborers. Recruits from miscellaneous or unknown professions made up 21 percent of the unit. Only two out of 1,083 members of the regiment over the years 1861–65 called themselves "planters," giving lie to the idea that the Southern Army was basically drawn from plantation owners (although 17 percent of the 3rd Texas Cavalry came from the planter or professional class). One man in the 1st Texas Cavalry gave his profession as "buffalo hunter."

It would be wrong, however, to assume that cavalrymen came from the same agrarian, poor class from which most infantrymen were drawn. Generally speaking, the cavalry drew men from the better-off sections of society, since each man had to provide a horse and equipment to serve. For example, the average household worth of each officer and man in the 3rd Texas Cavalry was $12,812, twice the household worth of the average Texas resident. Some 40 percent came from households that owned as many as 19 slaves. The average member of the regiment came from a household that owned eight slaves. Around a third of the regiment's men came from households owning more than 80 acres of land.

Most of the men in the 1st Texas were also native Southerners, with 58 percent coming from Southern states and another eight percent were from slave-owning border states. In the 3rd Texas, 60 percent of men came from the lower South, while 30 percent came from slave-owning border states. Texas was home to a larger than average number of German immigrants, and those born overseas or in Mexico made up 21 percent (103 were Germans out of 175 born overseas). Only 14 percent were born in Northern, free states. The men ranged in age from a bottom limit of 13 and an upper limit of 58, and in size from 4 ft 10 in. to 6 ft 4 in. (the latter soldier was born in Rhode Island; so much for "tall Texas tales").

RIGHT **Officers, such as First Lieutenant Philip B. Jones, adjutant, 10th Kentucky Cavalry, tended to wear the regulation double-breasted frock coat whenever possible, even though the jacket was also used while on campaign. (John Sickles collection)**

A mounted sentinel, drawn from life by Edwin Forbes, shows clearly a typical mounted cavalryman, with saber on left and carbine hanging from a carbine sling from left shoulder to right side. (*Military Images* magazine)

One regimental member later recalled that, "Almost every existing condition of existing society was represented upon our muster-rolls the moral and the immoral the Christian Deist the scholar and the illiterate, shoulder to shoulder without distinction of nationality or creed bound together by a tie of mutual interest and patriotism."

Officers were generally somewhat older then their men. Three-quarters of the enlisted men of the 9th Texas Cavalry, for example, were between 18 and 27, while the average age of the regiment's officers was 34. The youngest officer was 19, while the oldest was 53. Usually such older men resigned after a fairly short time in the field, due to exhaustion, and, in this case, the older officer went home after less than a year of service.

In the spring of 1862 the army was basically dissolved as one-year enlistments came to an end. The Confederate Congress essentially drafted those who did not volunteer for the duration of the war, but this draft could be avoided by re-enlisting. However, men did not have to re-enlist in their old units. Indeed, a number of infantrymen, seeing better duty in the other two branches, especially the cavalry, chose to switch. An infantry private from the 1st Maryland Infantry Regiment of 1861, on the end of his enlistment, went to Staunton, Virginia, where he bought a horse. He then joined Co. A, Maryland Cavalry, which, he reported "was composed chiefly of men who had been in the infantry for a year …" The unit was merged into the 2nd Virginia Cavalry.

Some men resorted to illegal methods of transfer. Stonewall Brigade Veteran John O. Casler, in the hospital in late 1864, recalled:

> In a few days we had orders to move the hospital to Staunton, and as I was fit for duty I got my discharge to report to Company A, 33rd Virginia Infantry. But, as I was familiar with the hospital office, I got some blank discharges and filled one out to suit myself, which was to report to Company D, 11th Virginia Cavalry, Rosser's Brigade.

The 1st Virginia Cavalry as drawn during the 1862 Maryland Campaign by an artist for *Harper's Weekly* who was captured during the campaign, although he was later released to publish this drawing. The officers and men still wear jackets with black trim, issued in 1861, but they would later wear the usual plain gray jackets and trousers. (*Military Images* magazine)

Men in other branches of the service were disdainful of the cavalry. Private O.P. Hargis, 1st Georgia Cavalry, later wrote, "The infantry didn't like the cavalry and as we passed along by them a little fellow with his knapsack on his back looked up at me and said you humped-back cavalry, you think you are very fine. Show me some of your sort and I will show you some of mine." Visiting Coldstream Guards Lieutenant-colonel Arthur Fremantle recorded that in 1863, "The infantry and artillery of this army [of Northern Virginia] don't seem to respect the cavalry very much, and often jeer at them." Cavalrymen generally ignored these jeers, feeling delighted to avoid walking. One Texas Ranger wrote home, on learning of a friend who had recently received an infantry commission, "I wood [*sic*] rather be corporal in company F of the Texas Rangers than to be a first Leiu in a flat foot company."

Training

New companies were organized into regiments at Camps of Instruction. Few of the recruits had any military experience, so there was much to learn. For example, the new sergeant-major of the 3rd Texas Cavalry one day asked his colonel, "What is my rank?"

The colonel replied, "Rank? You haven't any rank."

"Well, I resign," the sergeant-major said.

"You have nothing to resign, Mr. Warren," the colonel said.

"Can't resign! Well, in the name of God, what am I anyway?"

The colonel replied: "You are a waiting boy for headquarters, and at odd times hold the colonel's horse."

With that the sergeant-major told the colonel he "could take the damn little office and give it to some other fellow that wanted it."

Initially there were not enough drill manuals available, but eventually most new officers learned the complicated maneuvers from column into line and vice versa, as well as basic saber skills. The all-purpose volunteer soldier's manual, which was produced by Virginia Military Institute professor William Gilham, eventually became widely available in the South and was the most used system of tactics. It covered basic drill, saber techniques, and it showed the soldier how to ride in column and line, and how to attack and defend. Once officers had studied the manual, they could pass on essential information to their new soldiers.

One member of the new 1st Texas Cavalry wrote that, "Our duties were monotonous. Drilling in both cavalry and infantry drill from two to four hours per day was the usual routine to which a civilian soon becomes exceeding irksome."

Drill, however, was not stressed by all officers. Turner Ashby, the first leader of Virginia cavalry in the Valley of Virginia, was

This cartoon of a cavalry officer nodding off in a Richmond hotel bar appeared in the *Southern Illustrated News* of August 1, 1863.

notorious for his lack of attention to drill. Indeed, Major General Thomas ("Stonewall") Jackson complained on May 5, 1862:

> When I took steps for organizing, drilling and disciplining the cavalry, both of its field officers sent in their resignations; and such was Colonel Ashby's influence over his command that I became well satisfied that if I persisted in my attempt to increase the efficiency of the cavalry, it would produce the contrary effect, as Colonel Ashby's influence, who is very popular with his men, would be thrown against me.

Indeed, according to Ashby's ordnance officer, Captain William McDonald, "He taught his men that war meant getting close to the enemy, and requiring him to fight for every foot of the ground he attempted to advance upon; a lesson, if choice had to be made, of far more importance than dress parades and regimental maneuvers."

Surprisingly, since the men came with their own horses, many had to learn how to ride in a military manner so as to preserve horses for long marches. Charles Blackford, an officer with the 2nd Virginia Cavalry, wrote that the regiment's first march exhausted both men and horses:

> A great part of their discomfort and suffering arose from their inexperience in marching and in taking care of both men and horses: Many horses were rendered unfit for use by sore backs caused by awkward and unskilled riding. Some men can ride their horses for days and never injure their backs, while others will be seldom fit for duty on that account. The difference is in the manner they sit upon their horses and the mode of riding. A man who slouches down, rides with a swing, sits sometimes on one side and then on another, and never dismounts when the company halts, will always have a sore-backed horse.

As time went on, recalled Private Hopkins, "The cavalryman and his horse got very close to each other, not only physically, but heart to heart. They ate together, slept together, marched, fought and often died together. Frequently a wounded horse would be seen bearing his wounded rider back from the front."

Recruits also had to learn basic military discipline, and the Confederate cavalryman was never as good in this field as his opponent. Writing long after the war, however, Brigadier-General Thomas Rosser, commander of the Army of Northern Virginia's Laurel Brigade of cavalry, had a different memory. "My men were all good citizens, and consequently they were good soldiers and made a guard house in my command a useless thing," he wrote:

> I don't even remember even having a case of disobedience to deal with, and all orders given for the purpose of increasing the efficiency of the command were obeyed with the utmost alacrity. There was no murmuring or grumbling heard from the men, and while this is more than I can say of some officers, upon the whole, I think there was never in any service a finer, more cheerful and more efficient brigade than the "Old Laurel Brigade."

On the other hand, many cavalry units were known throughout the war as being less than perfectly disciplined. "This Texas brigade was one of the finest bodies of men ever seen in any service, but had no idea of accurate discipline. Their colonel was a very handsome, poetical-looking young fellow, with a voice and manner gentle as a woman's, and the heart of a true soldier of Texas," wrote one general of a particular brigade under his command in 1862. "He had not then the least

Another scene of Manassas winter quarters. (Library of Congress)

conception of discipline; so I and my staff devoted ourselves to Ross's brigade, for every potato patch and green apple tree drew them from the ranks until we drove them back again."

All in all, the average Confederate cavalrymen spent little time in a Camp of Instruction. The first camps for the volunteers of 1861 existed while things were relatively peaceful, which meant that by mid-1861 all their soldiers were in the field. Thereafter, Camps of Instruction were set up in each state for that particular state's conscripts.

Each soldier would stay in camp only a couple of weeks and would not be given any advanced cavalry training. Indeed, his training once released to a line unit from the camp would be in the form of on-the-job training. In some ways this was just as well, since most cavalry fighting bore little resemblance to that described in the manuals. Combat was rarely on horseback, but more usually on the ground, with men fighting as light infantry, armed with carbines rather than sabers. In the western Confederate cavalry, sabers were rarely seen, while in the Army of Northern Virginia they were carried, but often strapped out of the way to the saddle rather than carried on the belt. The basic skirmish infantry tactics that the average Confederate cavalryman used were never taught in cavalry manuals.

Fitzgerald Ross, a professional cavalry officer of the Austrian hussars, visited the South in 1863 and described what he saw with a veteran's eye:

The cavalry here is very differently organized from the same branch of the service in Europe. They are, in fact, mounted infantry. Every man's horse is his own property, and that may be one reason why they prefer fighting on foot, as if a man loses his horse, and cannot get another, he has forthwith to join the infantry. Besides, there has been no time to put them through a regular cavalry drill, and teach the efficient use of the saber – the true arm of real cavalry – whilst with the use of the rifle they have been familiar from their earliest youth. To handle a rifle efficiently, of course, a man must dismount. On the whole, I think they have acted judiciously in taking their men as they found them, and not trying to establish the European system. Besides, the country is so wooded and broken up with high fences that opportunities for a regular cavalry-charge on a large scale seldom occur. Their horses are generally good, some exceedingly so, but not large. I understand they are very enduring, and will go through any amount of rough work.

UNIFORMS, EQUIPMENT AND WEAPONS

Uniforms

The regulation Confederate cavalryman's uniform included a double-breasted frock coat of gray wool with yellow standing collar and trousers, sky blue trousers with a yellow stripe down each leg for non-commissioned officers and officers, and a copy of the French képi with a dark blue band and yellow sides and top. Coats of non-commissioned officers were to be marked with yellow chevrons, points down on each sleeve indicating grade, while officers were to wear gold embroidered rank insignia on each collar; one, two, and three bars for lieutenants and the captain, and one, two, and three stars for the major through colonel. Officers were also to wear gold lace in the form of an Austrian knot on each sleeve, with one lace for lieutenants, two for captains, and three for field-grade officers. The same number of gold bars was to decorate the front, back, side, and tops of the kepis.

In fact, the uniform described above was little seen in the field, especially the enlisted version. For the first two years of the war men supplied their own uniforms, for which they were paid by the central government, or, in the case of North Carolina and Georgia, they came from state supplies that conformed to state dress regulations. Almost immediately the frock coat was replaced by a waist-length jacket, with a single row of buttons ranging in number from five to nine. By 1863 the central Confederate government took over supplying its troops from a number of clothing depots located around the country. Each depot, as it turned out, had its own unique style of jacket, but most were similar to the short jackets already worn. The system worked well, and, while there were times that Confederates were poorly clad, for the most part they were well and uniformly dressed, although instead of gray wool, the uniforms were more often made of jeans cloth, a mixture of wool and cotton, and colored with logwood dyes that soon faded to brown.

A 12th Virginia Cavalryman wrote home on April 17, 1863, "The government is making strenuous efforts to provide the army with clothing now so you need have no uneasiness on my account. One of our boys managed to

A typical Southern-made tin drum canteen. The US Army tin oval canteen, which was covered with wool or jeans cloth for insulation, was preferred. (*Military Images* magazine)

get a splendid suit with Virginia buttons on …" The regulation button had a Roman letter "C" on but was otherwise plain. However, as suggested, state buttons were often preferred when available.

Cavalrymen were fiercely proud of their branch of service, and many men tried to obtain yellow to trim their otherwise plain gray jackets. Louisiana cavalry Sergeant Edwin Fay wrote home in April 1864, "See if you cannot get me some more yellow trimming for cuffs and collar." In December 1863 Fay again wrote that, "We went to Mr. Thigpen's and I took my coats out to have the cuffs and collars trimmed with yellow flannel (Cavalry stripes)."

Equipment

Cavalrymen carried a variety of equipment to support them in the field and in battle. Each man received a waist belt on which was attached a holster, a small pouch to hold percussion caps for both his pistol and carbine, a cartridge box, and his saber. A wide leather sling with a brass buckle also had an iron sling-swivel attached, from which was suspended the carbine. He carried his food in a haversack, which was either worn from shoulder to hip or attached to the saddle. Many men carried two canteens, one on their bodies for themselves, and another slung from the saddle for the horse in an emergency. Saddlebags held spare clothing.

Versions of all of this equipment were made in the South by local manufacturers. Southern versions, however, were considered inferior to Northern-made US Army versions of the same equipment. For example, the South was only able to make wood or tin drum canteens. These broke fairly easily, with the tops of the wooden versions breaking almost immediately the corks were rammed into them. The more durable US Army tin version, however, was covered with wool or jeans cloth that helped keep the water inside cool. In the same way, the Southern-made haversack was generally plain duck cotton, while the US Army haversack was made with a detachable food bag inside and was, moreover, painted with a waterproofing to keep its contents dry in rain. Cavalrymen, who could ride for miles around a battlefield, could easily replace their Southern-made goods with US Army versions, and it has been noted that after 1862 it was rare to see Southern-made equipment used by front-line units.

Weapons

Southern-made weapons were generally inferior to Northern-made US Army weapons. Southern-made sabers, for example, differed from Northern-made edged weapons, in that the blades were often only single-fullered on either side, the fullers running out at top and bottom, or even flat, which made them weaker than US Army sabers. Blades were often not rolled, but beaten out by hand; as a result they were uneven and of mixed quality. Brass parts were often cast with faults and flaws, and close-fought battles frequently found the Confederates at a disadvantage because of the inferior quality of such weapons. John Gill, 2nd Virginia Cavalry, recalled his first mounted fight:

Private J.O. Sheppard, Co. F, 6th South Carolina Cavalry, wears a US Army issue mounted man's sword belt, with the attached cross belt. This belt, which was detachable, was little used in the field. (BGEN James Daniels collection/US Army Military History Institute)

Unfortunately for me, my saber, a poor specimen of Confederate iron, was soon bent and quite useless. I was attacked by three Yankees. I was fighting for my life, when kindly aid came from one of my comrades by the name of Nelson, who cut down two of my opponents, and at the third I made a right cut which missed him, and nearly unhorsed me.

I had only a moment to gather my thoughts, and in that moment my pistol was leveled at him, to surrender or die. He threw up his hands and surrendered – horse, foot and dragoon.

John S. Mosby recalled serving as a recruit in the 1st Virginia Cavalry in early 1861:

At Richmond, Captain Jones, who stood high with those in authority, had procured Sharp[s] carbines for us. We considered this a great compliment, as arms were scarce in the Confederacy. We had been furnished with sabers before we left Abingdon, but the only real use I ever heard of their being put to was to hold a piece of meat over a fire for frying. I dragged one through the first year of the war, but when I became a commander, I discarded it.

The saber was totally ignored by western cavalrymen. Isaac Affleck, Terry's Texas Rangers, wrote home on March 21, 1862 that he "shot both barrels of my gun [obviously a shotgun] at a crowd of yankeys in a lane about thirty yards distance." Five months later he wrote home for a pair of "Texas made six-shooters." An item in the *Austin Texas Almanac-Extra*, dated February 28, 1863, confirmed such weapons:

We were shown the other day a beautiful specimen of a six-shooter, manufactured near Dallas by Colonel Crockett, who has a large armory now in successful operation. The pistol appears in every respect quite equal to the famous Colt's six-shooter, of which it is an exact copy, with the exception of an extra sight on the barrel which we think is a decided improvement.

Confederate cavalrymen in the western theater of operations. Most have a revolver thrust into their belt rather than a holster and all have carbines and sabers.
(Miller's *Photographic History*)

However, these pistols were often as inferior to Colt's Connecticut-made revolvers – and the other types of Northern-made revolvers – as were Confederate edged weapons. As iron was always in short supply in the Confederacy, many had brass frames which tended to wear out, exposing a gap between the cylinder and barrel over time; this made them more dangerous, as escaping gas could set off the other rounds in the cylinder upon use. On a test of 22 pistols produced by one of the leading Southern makers of revolvers, Griswold and Gunnison, in October 1862, the army inspector reported: "The barrels of three of the pistols bursted. One was found deficient because of a defect in the casting of the base, another because of a broken hand spring, another for a bursted tube or cone and another because the ramrod catch was broken off." Other rejects were caused by untempered springs and bolts.

The main problem, however, with Southern-made handguns was that few were manufactured due to a lack of local manufacturing capabilities, raw materials, and trained machinists. The Confederate cavalryman, therefore, depended on obtaining Northern-made revolvers as his main handgun.

Louisiana cavalryman Edwin Fay wrote home in April 1862, "I bought me a large sized Colt's revolver [for] which I paid $55 as I was determined to be as well armed as any of the company and if I could buy another I would do it to carry in my holsters." In November 1863 he wrote home:

> Did I tell you about some body stealing my pistol, belt, cap box and all. I had $1.50 waterproof [percussion] caps that I was going to send [home]. The pistol was worth $125.00. So you see I had some bad luck. If I come over I shall buy me another, if not don't want any. Shall send a Smith's patent [carbine] by Lt. Watkins if I cannot exchange it for a Maynard [carbine].

The Governor of Alabama wrote the Secretary of War to get weapons for his cavalry and received this reply, dated March 17, 1862:

> I have, however, no sabers or pistols of the latter, even our rich enemies are destitute. Cavalry is found most efficient with double-barreled guns, and cavalry officers report that after a month or two sabers are universally discarded as useless, men not being thoroughly trained to the use of that arm.

Weapons carried by western cavalry units, however, were generally of less quality than those issued in the east. The 1st Texas Cavalry reported in December 1863, that its members carried 54 muskets, 253 Enfield rifles, 53 carbines and musketoons, 100 0.54-caliber M1854 "Mississippi" rifles, 47 "minie" muskets, 16 shotguns, 28 Sharps rifles, 51 revolvers, 28 sporting rifles, three pairs of holster pistols, and 13 "Harper's Ferry" rifles; possibly breechloaders from the Mexican War-period. An inspection of the 3rd Texas Cavalry in August 1861 showed three companies armed with single-shot percussion pistols and shotguns, five companies armed with the same pistols plus M1841 percussion rifles, and two companies armed with the same pistols and Sharps carbines.

First Lieutenant J.H. Wells, 7th Kentucky Cavalry, is armed with both regulation saber and revolver. (John Sickles collection)

The one thing most cavalrymen did have, initially at least, was a large knife. Lieutenant R.M. Collins, 15th Texas Cavalry, recalled:

> In one thing only were all armed alike, and that was with big knives. These were made for us by the blacksmiths, out of old scythe blades, plowshares, crosscut saws, or anything else that could be had. The blade was from two to three feet in length, and ground as sharp as could be. The scabbards for these great knives were, as a rule, made of raw hide, with the hairy side out, and they were worn on the belt like a sword, and doubtless many trees in the pine forests over in Arkansas show to this day the marks of these knives, for we used to mount our ponies and gallop through pine thickets, cutting the tops from young pine trees, practicing so that we could lift the heads of the Yankees artistically as soon as we could catch up with them.

These knives proved useless in combat and of limited use in camp, and most were either sent home or sold shortly after the owner entered the service.

Most of the men arrived with a variety of longarms. Private A.W. Sparks, 9th Texas Cavalry, wrote that most of the first men had:

> rifles, flint and steel, but most were full stock percussion muzzle-loading machines that had been used for killing bear, deer and other wild animals. Double-barrel shotguns were the favorite. A few pistols were in the command, and were in great demand by the officers. Each soldier carried a huge knife, usually made from an old mill file, shaped by the blacksmith and ground according to the fancy of the owner.

The knives would soon be discarded, while issue carbines, revolvers, and sabers would replace the weapons brought from home, which were usually sent back home for use there. As Charles Blackford, an officer in the 2nd Virginia Cavalry recalled, "It was supposed the shotgun would be an efficient arm but it was too frail and was soon abandoned. After first battle of Manassas we supplied ourselves with the captures of the enemy and had good carbines for the rest of the war."

Confederate cavalrymen were issued a variety of carbines. One was a patented Maynard carbine, about which an English visitor to the Confederacy quoted a cavalryman as saying:

> [The Maynard carbine] is the favorite with us, and proves a destructive weapon when one become accustomed to handling it, mounted, in a skirmish. It is light, simple in structure, and can be used with both caps; the only objection is that you have to be careful in preserving the empty brass tubes, or you will not be able to make new cartridges. I wear a belt around me which holds fifty, each in its hole, ready for use, but I object to the brass tubes, for, if lost, it is difficult to replace them in active service.

About 280 Maynard carbines were actually produced by Keen, Walker & Co., Danville, Virginia. The carefully machined brass cartridges required for the Maynard and referred to by the cavalryman, were difficult even to make in the Confederacy, and as such limited the use of not only this carbine, but also captured Federal models, such as the Spencer and Henry.

Captured carbines were, nevertheless, pressed into service whenever possible. Colonel R.H. Dulany, 7th Virginia Cavalry, reported after one 1864 battle, "We had a number of the Henry sixteen-shooters recently captured from Wilson's cavalry, and our fire was so rapid that Hill (the ememy commander) became uneasy, supposing we had run up against infantry." Generally, however, such carbines had limited use, whereas breechloaders using paper cartridges such as the Sharps and the Starr, were much preferred.

As with revolvers, the Confederates tried to make copies of Northern-made breech-loading carbines. A factory was opened in Richmond in 1862 and began production of copies of these favored Union weapons that December. In March 1863 the first weapons reached front-line units, and shortly thereafter Lieutenant N.D. Morris' men in the 4th Virginia test-fired them. Morris reported the results to a Richmond newspaper: "Forty new Sharps rifles with Richmond stamp on them were handed yesterday to my company. The men were ordered to test them. Nine were fired, and seven of the nine burst."

As is so often the case, those in charge blamed the testers rather than the weapon. On April 3 the Superintendent of the Richmond Armory wrote:

> I have no hesitation in saying that there is a misunderstanding or a mistake of some kind in this statement. In the first place, this being a breech-loading arm, it is impossible to introduce a sufficient charge of ammunition into the gun to burst it unless the muzzle is plugged up intentionally … Again; these barrels are all proven with a charge five times greater than the service charge before they are passed by the inspector. I have no doubt that injury to the arms has arisen from the ignorance of the men in handling a weapon which was new to them, and in which they have been uninstructed by their officers.

At the same time, however, a report went to the manufacturer: "Capt. J. Esten Cooke, Chief of Ordnance, Cavalry Division, reports to Col. J. Gorgas that your carbine seems to be regarded as an excellent weapon, but not perfectly put together."

To ensure quality control, the Confederate government took over the carbine factory in March 1863. Prior to that point, some 1,800 carbines had been produced, and the government continued to turn out around 500 carbines a month until the spring of 1864, producing a total of about 5,000.

Other private manufacturers produced breech-loading carbines for the Confederate cavalry. Bilharz, Hall and Co., Chatham, Virginia, turned out a so-called "rising block" model in which the operator brought the trigger guard down to shove the block up so a new paper round could be inserted.

Private John P. Sellman, Co. K, 1st Virginia Cavalry, has a regulation issue US Army mounted man's sword belt, with the cross belt missing, and a percussion cap box on his right front hip in front of the usual holster, worn butt out. (Charles T. Jacobs/US Army Military History Institute)

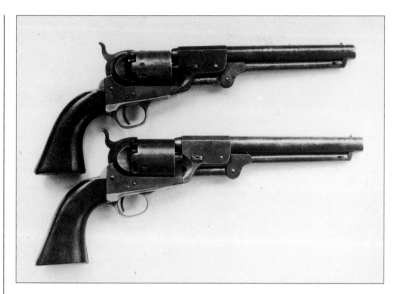

A pair of Southern-made copies of the Colt 0.36-caliber "Navy" revolver. The top one was produced by Rigdon-Ansley, after January 1864, in Augusta, Georgia, while the bottom one was made by Leech & Rigdon, between mid-1862 and December 1863.
(Russ Pritchard collection)

These guns were made in small numbers from August 1862 through March 1864. The highest serial number known is 353. A few hundred Tarpley breech-loading carbines were also made by the J. and F. Garrett Co., Greensboro, North Carolina, in 1863–64. The State Military Works, Greenville, South Carolina, produced around 1,000 Morse Carbines that used a 0.50-caliber brass cartridge round, which was difficult to supply in the South. These carbines were mostly used by South Carolina's militia cavalry.

In fact, the most common Southern-made carbines were actually little more than cut-down copies of the infantry's rifled muskets. These guns were produced in large numbers on machinery captured at the burned-down Harper's Ferry Armory and brought to Richmond for use in the Confederate Armory. The ease of ammunition re-supply, as well as low cost of manufacture, caused Robert E. Lee to request that the Ordnance Department prepare such a weapon as the standard model for his cavalry in July 1863. The department's experts designed a model based closely on the British Enfield carbine, and it was adopted on October 31, 1863. Now the department had to pick a place to manufacture such a weapon, and after considering several sites, picked Tallahassee, Alabama, where water power was available and transportation links were good, but which was also safe from Federal raiders.

The factory was set up throughout 1864 and the first 500 carbines were finally ready for shipment as of April 3, 1865. A week later, however, Lee surrendered his Army of Northern Virginia, and other Confederate armies quickly followed suit. The standard carbines never saw active service.

EVERYDAY LIFE

A visitor to a Texas cavalry brigade camp in 1862 described a typical camp scene at that point in the war:

> … innumerable white tents. Look into the cavalry officers' tents, and you will find that they don't fare so badly in camp. Neat beds are contrived; some are cots, others saplings or frames covered with cotton, and plenty of coverings. On one side is a table, with books and novels, a box of cigars, and, most likely, a bottle of "commissary." These, with a looking-glass, and the officers' equipments are complete. Four flies form a mess-tent; and as the colonel and staff are going to dine, we will just see what kind of fare they have. It consists of stewed beef, boiled ham, mashed

potatoes, and a couple of chickens, which some of the Austin County housekeepers were kind enough to raise for them – *at least the officers' servants thought so*; for dessert, a couple of bottles of old rye, which some of the planters sent them – for their especial benefit; all these flanked by a respectable force of negro waiters.

Officers and orderlies are always lounging or riding about headquarters, which gave it a very gay and stirring appearance. At some distance from the colonel's headquarters are the less pretentious headquarters of some of his subordinate officers, while, a little further on, are the modest tents of the rank and file, arranged in streets.

The men around these [tents] are collected in groups, wearing their bell-spurs, which around each waist is dangling a huge knife, made by some village blacksmith, giving them the appearance of warriors, apparently ready for any emergency. Some are playing cards, pitch and toss, or a thousand other games known only in the army; others are dining, and grumbling at their rations, while dining, perhaps, on turkey. The cooks are busy around a huge camp-kettle, placed on the fire, in which a joint of bacon and some peas are bubbling and bubbling around, as if they were patriotic enough to enjoy being eaten for the good of the soldier. A smaller vessel simmers near it; but, as the lid is on it, I cannot see its contents – most likely a brace of chickens under the wing of a fat turkey. This is the way the cavalry lived at "Camp Hebert."

Cavalry officers and men also enjoyed racing their horses, placing bets on the results. "I have bin Horse racesing since I left home," a Texan wrote home in 1862. "I have Lost one hundred dollars and have got arace to be run on Saturday next I have got dick [his horse] bet on the race and if I loose him I will loose aheap more on the day of the race. I am going to win or loose something." Such events were so commonplace among cavalrymen that the commander of the Texas Frontier Regiment issued orders on June 17, 1863 ordering all his officers "to prohibit gaming by horse racing … whenever the same in any company or detachment shall become a nuisance to the service."

While camp life sounds pleasant enough, disease soon appeared in most Confederate camps and the men, many of whom grew up in isolated farms and were therefore not resistant to ailments such as measles and mumps, died easily. By the middle of October 1861 in camp in Missouri, a third of the 3rd Texas Cavalry were too sick for duty with measles and, later, typhoid. Foul water brought the

The US Army's contract revolver, a 0.45-caliber Colt "Army," was the preferred Confederate cavalry handgun.
(Chris Nelson collection)

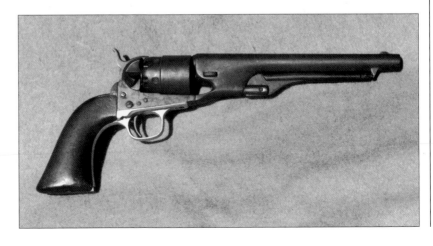

latter disease, as well as dysentery. Poor diets also contributed, causing diarrhea which often became chronic and led to an early discharge from service.

Camps later became more simple as tents disappeared among Confederate enlisted men, and many officers as well. Private Hopkins, 6th Virginia Cavalry, recalled the winter of 1862–63 as a:

> hard one … We had no tents, but took fence rails, and putting one end on a pole fastened to two trees, and the other on the ground, and covering the rails with leaves and fastening up each end, leaving the front open, then building a big fire just in front, we had a very comfortable place to sleep. We sat on logs around the fire during the day and far into the night telling stories and entertaining ourselves in various ways. At night we crept under the roof of our shed, which was about a foot deep in leaves, and slept as comfortably as any farmer's hogs would do under similar circumstances.

Each hut would hold a small, informal group that had banded together for mutual protection. As Private Hopkins recalled:

> The men in the companies are always divided into messes; the average number of men in each was usually about six. The messes were like so many families that lived together, slept together and ate together, and stood by each other in all emergencies. There was no rule regulating the messes. The men simply came together by common consent. "Birds of a feather flock together."
>
> In winter one bed was made for the whole mess. It consisted of laying down rubber cloths on the ground and covering them with a blanket, and another and another, as occasion required, and if the weather was foul, on top of that other rubber cloths. Our saddles covered with our coats were our pillows. The two end men had logs of wood to protect them. Only our coats and boots were removed.

Confederates pressed a wide variety of captured US Army weapons into use. One of the more obscure was the Butterfield revolver, which used a patented pellet primer device. (Chris Nelson collection)

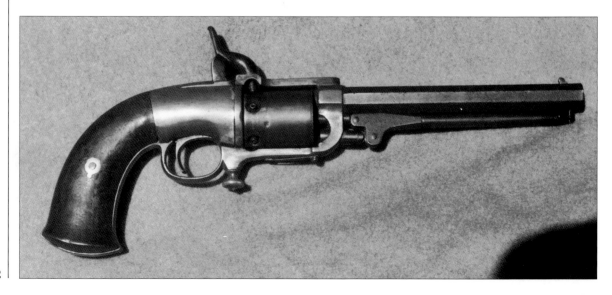

Many winter camps tended to be in the South, near friendly civilians, so soldiers often took advantage of local social events. Dances were frequently held in farmhouses and halls and cavalrymen could bring their local girlfriends with them. One 3rd Texas Cavalry private recalled that "along toward the close of night ... each fellow would take his girl up behind him on his steed, and after delivering her at her house, hie himself away to camp in time to answer 'here' at roll call."

Southerners were from a society that was heavily Protestant. The Rev. Randolph McKim, a newly ordained Episcopal priest, joined the 2nd Virginia Cavalry as regimental chaplain in time for the 1864 campaign. McKim stated that he, "established the rule of having prayers in the regiment daily, both morning and evening, and that I generally made a short address." He was exceptionally busy, recalling that he:

> rose regularly about five, sometimes half an hour earlier, groomed and fed my horse, and was early ready for any duty. If the regiment went on picket, prayers would first be held, unless it was very early, I believe the morning service was usually before breakfast and the evening service at sunset, though sometimes, especially, on Sunday it would be after dark ...

Rev. McKim also organized a choir for his service. In all, he concluded,

> I found these sturdy men very ready to discuss the great question of religion, and open to conviction. Even the gayest and most seemingly thoughtless would listen with deep attention. Danger and death were at their right hand very often, and this gave emphasis to the counsels and warnings I addressed to them in public and private.

The Reverend's duties also included setting up a branch of the Young Men's Christian Association in his regiment as well as distributing religious reading matter whenever possible.

> One of my efforts was to supply all the men who wished it with copies of the New Testament. To this end I appointed one [man] in each company to ascertain how many were desirous of being supplied with them. I also circulated a subscription for the supply of "religious papers," and I note November 14th the receipt of $106 from Co. A for this purpose.

Food also grew scarce during the war, and cavalrymen even ate some of their supplied horses' feed. Private Hopkins wrote that:

> during the winter months, when we needed some kind of beverage to wash down our hardtack, the only thing we could get was horse feed, which was roasted and boiled. We called it coffee. It was very good then. We had to rob our horses for this, and we all felt mean when we did it. A tablespoonfull, however, was all that each man had to take from his horse for a cup of coffee.

When corn was ripe man and animal also shared, although, as Hopkins pointed out, "We cooked ours, while the horse took his green."

Confederate cavalrymen generally had life much easier in garrison than did their counterparts in the infantry, artillery, or engineers. Cavalrymen were free to ride out of camp and forage from the countryside, while foot troops were forced to stay either in camp or on their line of march, where chances to forage were few. As a result, cavalrymen were generally better fed than the rest of the army. John Gill, 2nd Virginia Cavalry, recalled how the men "amused ourselves, when out on picket duty, by shooting partridges and different kinds of game." Infantrymen and artillerymen rarely had the same chance of supplementing their rations.

John Porter, 1st Kentucky Cavalry, recalled that the cavalryman:

These two members of the 6th Virginia Cavalry have their revolvers thrust into their belts. The man on the left has a Colt M1851 "Navy" revolver, while his friend has a 0.31-caliber M1849 5-shot Colt revolver. (Library of Congress)

had no need for money, like a poor Infantry soldier, who was confined to his camp and obliged to eat what was in hand. He could use money to buy things from sutlers and others. A horseman could ride around till he found a place where he could get a "good meal," as we called it. There were many advantages to being a Cavalryman, as the Infantry arm of the service, were confined for weeks and months to camp, by reason of which diseases were contracted. The Cavalry was mostly on the wing, and activity plus exercise were more healthy.

Sutlers were individuals who were authorized to sell small items such as canned food, boot black, and sewing and writing equipment to a specific regiment. Generally such items were so rare in the South, and the mobile retail tradition was so uncommon among Southerners, that sutlers were rare. There were some, however, who served specific units throughout the war. Even in late 1864 Rev. McKim wrote that he "rebuked the sutlers for selling their merchandise on the Lord's Day …"

Soldiers also had a chance to stop by inns and stores on their lines of march and buy food. But pay rates were low: A private received $11 a month; a musician, corporal, farrier, or blacksmith received $13; a sergeant, $17; a first sergeant, $20; a sergeant-major, $21; a second lieutenant, $90; a first lieutenant, $100; a captain, $140; a major, $162; a lieutenant-colonel, $185; and a colonel, $210. As an attempt to meet rising costs due to inflated paper currency, all enlisted men received a pay raise of $7 a month as of June 1864. As the war progressed, however, paper money declined in value tremendously.

By 1863 a pair of boots cost a private ten months' pay, while even a chicken cost the equal of four days' pay. McKim recalled, "In December,

1864, I bought 6 pounds butter for $54, 1 turkey, $17, 1 spool cotton, $5, soap, $2 per pound. In January, 1865, 1 yard mourning crepe cost $140, putting one shoe on my horse, $5."

As a result of this impossible inflation, many cavalrymen felt justified in looting whatever they could. Indeed, the cavalry got such a bad reputation among civilians as a result, that North Carolina Governor Z.B. Vance wrote Richmond in December 1863, "If God Almighty had yet in store another plague worse than all others which he intended to have let loose on the Egyptians in case Pharaoh still hardened his heart, I am sure it must have been a regiment or so of half-armed, half-disciplined Confederate Cavalry."

However, much of the cavalry's seemingly unsociable behavior was understandable, since they were used as couriers and as pickets, serving as the eyes and ears of the army in the field. They had to scout enemy positions at all time to make sure that the Union army wasn't doing something that could trap the Confederate forces. Such activity kept them out legitimately at all times of the day and night, during all seasons. If the cavalryman found a warm barn to sleep in and civilians to share their tables with him, it seemed to him only to be fair.

The cavalryman also had the additional responsibility of caring for his horse. At this time, horse care was still a do-it-yourself type of operation. No trained veterinarians were appointed in cavalry units. The most professional veterinary care came from blacksmiths and farriers, with a limited number of "horse doctors" available, most of whom lacked professional training. Indeed, before the 1850s the only professionally trained veterinarians had been educated in Europe. In America there were only a handful of professional schools established before the war, including the Veterinary College of Philadelphia, founded in 1852; the Boston Veterinary Institute, founded in 1855; and the New York College of Veterinary Surgeons, founded in 1857. The Ohio Agricultural College began offering lectures in veterinary medicine to anyone interested in 1855, as did two other local colleges, but none offered a degree in the subject.

Most American schools, by contrast, tended to be diploma mills; a degree from the average veterinary school in Philadelphia in 1877, for example, cost only $100. Students needed no more than an eighth-grade education for admittance and rarely had to attend lectures. There was no licensing system to assure professional medical care for horses, and as a result the Confederate Army did not recognize such a profession as deserving an official position.

Most horse owners depended on publications such as the 1859 *American Horse Tamer and Farrier,*

Richmond firm, S.C. Robinson, produced copies of the Sharps breech-loading carbine for the Confederate Army. These weapons received a reputation for being poorly assembled from low quality parts. Unsurprisingly, soldiers disliked using them. (Russ Pritchard collection)

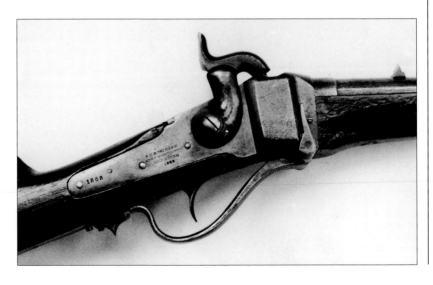

which offered "remedies for all diseases to which horses are liable; such as spavin, distemper, ringbone, etc.," and the 1846 book, *The Veterinary Surgeon or Farrier. Taught on a New and Easy Plan.* Such publications rarely offered very good advice. For example, bleeding, something abandoned for human patients, was recommended for such ailments as blind staggers, colic, or dysentery. Treatments, involving as much as a quart or two of blood drained from a horse's neck, sometimes so weakened the animal that death was inevitable.

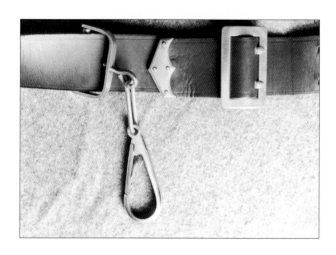

An iron hook attached the carbine to the sling, as shown here. (*Military Images* Magazine)

Red-hot irons used to burn or blister an animal were used for mouth and bone ailments, such as lampas, a congestion of the mucus membrane of the hard palate. Spavin and ringbone were treated by burning the diseased portion of the bone, using neatsfoot oil afterward to dress the wound. Brandy and salt were poured into the ears of horses with staggers, while a frog, with its left leg carefully removed, was mixed with salt and ale and fed to a horse to eliminate blood from the urine.

Even healthy horses had to be fed, watered, and groomed daily. This responsibility called for the cavalryman to be away from camp or the line of march often. Keeping a sufficient supply of forage for all the army's horses, which included not only those of the cavalry but also the wagon train and artillery, was very difficult for a Confederate commissary system that depended on a poor transportation network. For example, to supply a company of 85 cavalrymen, along with 30 additional mules and pack horses needed for company supplies, would take 31,050 pounds of grain per month, with an additional 44,850 pounds required in the winter.

All the additional water needed by the other branches often called for the cavalryman to travel great distances from the army.

A trooper from the Laurel Brigade recorded in his diary in 1864:

May 14th. Lay still all day; no rations. Ewell is at Frederich Hall.

15th. Crossed North Anna at Caws Bridge, moved along very slowly, reached our stopping place after dark, and fooled around till late hunting grass. No rations yet.

16th. Drew two crackers and a little meat; nothing for the horses. Marched all day on the country roads; borrowed a few rations from another command for us. No corn tonight and not a particle of grass; camped after dark.

17th. Grazed the horses a little this morning; wagons with corn and rations expected, but no one seems to know anything definite about them. The dust is three inches deep everywhere, and the sun boiling hot.

18th. No wagons yet, the men are suffering very much for rations, and have been for several days. Drew plenty of corn. Moved back on Wickham's Farm on the Pamunkey River, where we found the long expected wagons with four days' rations. Two squadrons have been without rations since the 12th.

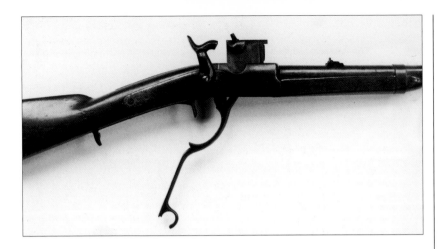

A "rising breech" carbine as produced by Bilharz, Hall and Co., Chatham, Virginia. A serial number of 353 suggests that a considerable number of these weapons were produced and put into service.
(Russ Pritchard collection)

By the winter of 1864–65 conditions throughout the South had deteriorated as transportation systems broke down, making bringing up food for the men and forage for the horses more and more difficult. Ground around cantonment areas was swept clean of anything of use. "I have pulled dried grass in December for my horse until my fingers bled," wrote Private Hopkins.

As McDonald wrote of the Laurel Brigade camp in that winter: "hope and fortitude would not feed and clothe the men, nor keep alive the horses, upon which the usefulness of cavalry so much depends. Day by day the brigade was diminishing in numbers. Many went home, by permission, after fresh horses; many took 'French leave,' not as deserters, but for temporary absence without furlough."

Many others, however, just voted themselves out of the service and went home to stay. Desertion rates rose tremendously as the war went on and Federal forces took more and more Southern land. On the night of September 3, 1863, for example, 31 men and an officer deserted from the 9th Texas Cavalry. In the same area, 19 soldiers from the 3rd Texas Cavalry deserted between August 1 and October 30, 1863. It was a problem the Confederacy never solved.

CAMPAIGN LIFE

The highlight of the cavalryman's life was the raid, and it was in raiding that the Confederate cavalry was mostly used. In the west, cavalry under Forrest, Morgan, and Wheeler struck repeatedly at Union supply lines, forcing Union commanders to make changes in their strategies. Grant had to abandon his attack on Vicksburg from the north, picking a route that would take him south of the city on the Mississippi River, because of a major raid on his supply center at the start of his first try at a campaign there. In the east, Stuart's cavalry entirely encircled the Army of the Potomac during the Peninsula Campaign in 1862, bringing back information to Robert E. Lee that allowed him to begin his Seven Days Campaign that took the pressure off Richmond.

These raids were stressful events. The men spent up to 20 hours at a time in the saddle. "There were many times when the cavalry would march all night," Private Hopkins wrote:

The men soon learned to sleep on horseback, or you might call it nodding, but some went sound asleep sitting upright on their horses. Occasionally, when a soldier was caught fast asleep, his comrade would slip the rein out of his hand and lead his horse to a fence corner and hitch it. The sudden stopping would awaken him, for he would at once begin to fall.

Food was only that which the men could bring or find along the way. Confederate cavalrymen generally had to be on the alert, since their Union counterparts were always in pursuit. The situation was made no easier by telegraphs that warned enemy troops ahead of their presence, giving them time to prepare for an attack. Men had very specific duties during these raids. Stuart even brought a trained telegraph operator to tap into telegraph lines on the way and gather intelligence on the enemy.

On the positive side, raids were also a way of finding food and other items not available in camp, which made them something to be anticipated. John Blue, 17th Virginia Cavalry Battalion, recalled how on a march in 1863:

> some of the boys winded a still house where persimmon lightening was manufactured. Three of four men from each company quietly gathered all the canteens in their company and quietly dropped out of ranks and did not reach camp until perhaps ten o'clock that night.
>
> Next morning at roll call about one half of our company failed to answer to their names. While this kind of lightning was not as fatal as genuine, it was for a time just as effective as far as locomotion was concerned. Quite a number of the boys were very much demoralized, but we succeeded in getting all into camp that night at Gordonsville.

At other times, cavalry was used not to raid, but to screen the main army from nosy Union cavalry scouts. Again, the cavalryman had to spend long hours in the saddle, alert to enemy troops at all times. As in the raid, the only advantage was that the cavalryman had a chance to forage liberally from civilians on his way. The men also traveled lightly in terms of camping equipment. As Private Hopkins, 6th Virginia Cavalry, recalled, "In the summer each soldier had a separate bed. If it were raining, he made his bed on top of two fence rails, if he could not find a better place. If the weather was good, old Mother Earth was all the soldier wanted."

The 0.50-caliber metallic center-fire cartridge required by this Morse Carbine, made by the Greenville Military Works for South Carolina's militia, was difficult to produce in the South, making the value of this weapon somewhat limited. (Russ Pritchard collection)

Rev. McKim recalled:

Every man was supposed to have a small tent-fly rolled up behind him. These were about six feet long and perhaps eighteen inches across, – two of them buttoned together and stretched across a small pole cut from the forest and supported by two forked sticks formed a little shelter under which two men could crawl and have some protection from falling weather.

The cavalryman's horse was not far away from where he slept. Private Hopkins wrote:

Much of the time, while in Pennsylvania, the men slept with their horses tied to the wrist. While the rider slept, the horse cropped the grass around his body as far out as his tether would allow, and as close up to his rider's body as he could get. Sometimes he would push the man's head aside with his nose to get the grass beneath it. I have seen men by the thousands lying in this manner in the fields with their horses grazing about them, yet I never knew a horse to tread on one, or in any way injure him.

On one occasion, Private Hopkins saw a man asleep whose horse, "had closely cropped the grass all around him, and as far out as he could reach, and so completely had he taken every spear of grass about the soldier that when the man got up he left a perfect outline of his body on the field."

Many generals in the field felt that they had too many cavalry, both to serve their battle needs and to supply their horses with forage. Entire cavalry regiments were dismounted, much to the dismay of their members, who often threatened to desert as a group and return home until returned to the mounted cavalry. The 10th Texas, for example, was dismounted after seeing some mounted service in Corinth, Mississippi, and some of its members were given the job of taking the unit's horses back to Texas. The men fought every way they could to get their horses restored, and eventually they were. Not all such units were so successful. In the Army of Northern Virginia in Petersburg in late 1864, when horse food was at a premium, Lee had a number of units dismounted to fight in the trenches as infantry, and they remained as infantry until the army's surrender.

On other occasions, there were so many men who had lost horses that they were put together into dismounted battalions. Major Edward McDonald,

This 0.52-caliber carbine was simple but effective. Keen, Walker & Co., Danville, Virginia, made 282 of these weapons before the war ended. (Russ Pritchard collection)

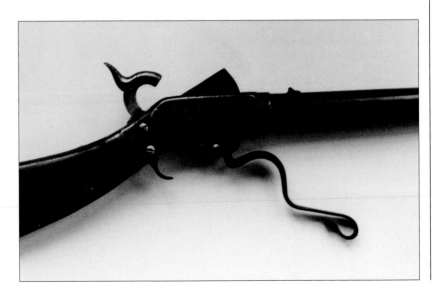

11th Virginia Cavalry, for example, reported that during the 1864 campaign to Petersburg:

> I was put in command of all the dismounted men of all the cavalry divisions, in numbers equal to a regiment [some 400 in all]. They had lost their horses but could not be spared from the army, so I was expected to organize them into companies, have officers detailed to command, organize my own commissary and quartermaster department, in fact form a separate command.
>
> It was an arduous task. These men had enlisted as cavalry and some of them declined to drill as infantry. All those who refused to drill, after I had stated to them the urgency and necessity of obeying General Lee's order, I had marched down to my headquarters. I told them that I was surprised that any Confederate soldier would refuse to do his duty in all and every condition of the service, and I hoped they would reconsider their determination. All who were willing to be infantry, temporarily, could return to the quarters. Those that refused would have to be punished.
>
> All but ten men promised to drill. The ten were ordered to march for two hours carrying rails. Two of the ten refused to carry the rails. I then threatened to have the two shot. One relented. The other was a Marylander and he said he would rather be shot than drill. He was a handsome young fellow, evidently spoiled by his parents. I relented and had him sent to General Lee with the charge of insubordination. He was confined in prison a long time, until I withdrew the charges and had him released. After this I had no more trouble with my infantry – had them well drilled.

As the war progressed, supply shortages continued to make Confederate cavalry less effective in the field. As Charles Blackford, originally from the 2nd Virginia Cavalry and then on James Longstreet's staff, wrote home on June 7, 1864:

> On our side our horses are worn down, and there is no source whence we can recruit. We have only pistols, sabers and old fashioned rifles, worn-out saddles, and none of the equipment in the way of portable furnaces, horse-shoes and transportation requisite for efficient cavalry work; and above all, we have not enough food to keep the horses up. Our cavalry is a very fine body of men, and we have some fine officers: Fitz Lee, Wickham, Rosser, Payne and others, but no horse can be kept efficient under the circumstances. The loss of a shoe from a horse where there is no convenient place to replace it, renders the cavalryman useless, and a horse unfed for several days is even more destructive.

In both the east and western theaters cavalrymen reported lulls in campaigns, during which soldiers on both sides met informally to trade goods, northern coffee for southern tobacco. Bands often serenaded both sides. Major McDonald remembered during the almost non-stop 1864 campaign to Petersburg, one such incident:

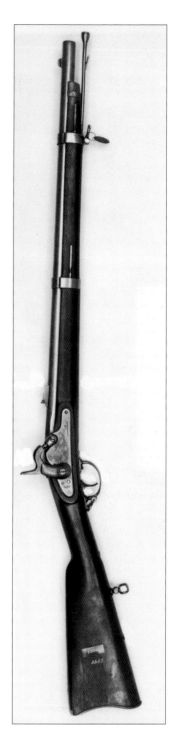

Two versions of the 0.58 caliber muzzle-loading carbine produced by the Confederate government in its Richmond Armory using machinery captured at the Harper's Ferry Arsenal at the beginning of the war. (Russ Pritchard collection)

One beautiful night during these terrible days I was sitting in the moonlight, looking up into the heavens so beautiful and calm – while everything around us which men controlled was full of evil and death – when the bands of the contending armies began to play. The Yankees played their national airs, and our side "Dixie," "The Bonnie Blue Flag," etc., while the armies listened and cheered the tunes of their side. One band struck up "Home Sweet Home," which was followed by others until all the bands of both sides joined in. Then the soldiers of both sides began to sing it, each gathering inspiration from the others, until all swelled the chorus, and the spirit of war was hushed as all hearts thought of the loved ones at home.

BATTLE

The ultimate use of cavalry was battle, and this tested the nerves of every cavalryman. Private Hopkins admitted that:

there is an atmosphere that hangs around the camp on the eve of an approaching battle that is well calculated to give one's imagination full play. The doctors examining their medical chests, packages of white bandages and lint arriving, the movement of the ambulances, the unusual number of litters that come into view, the chaplains a little more fervent in their prayers, officers, from the commanding general down to the lowest rank, more reserved and less approachable. Even the horses seem to be restive, or we imagine them to be so. In fact, everything takes on a different attitude. The very air appears to be laden with an indescribable something that makes every individual soldier feel himself lifted up into a position of responsibility quite different from the place he occupied while loitering around the camp with the enemy far away from the front.

Waiting was hard, especially when drawn up in line of battle, the enemy in sight, and enemy cannon fire falling into the ranks. Rev. McKim of the 2nd Virginia recalled one such time when, "The enemy was feeling for us with his artillery, and his shells were dropping uncomfortably near. I rode to the front of the squadron, drew out my little Psalm book, read the Twenty-seventh Psalm, and offered prayer for the divine blessing and protection, the men reverently removing their hats."

Traditionally the cavalry was saved for shock value in battle, dashing in when an enemy was weakened by friendly fire, and smashing their formations. The Confederate cavalry tried this tactic in action from time to time. At the First Manassas, Stuart's 1st Virginia Cavalry Regiment was called from the reserve in the height of the action and instructed simply to find a place and go in. Stuart saw a Union regiment of Zouaves supporting some artillery, and dashed his men forward in a traditional saber attack. In this case, the attack worked, and the Zouaves fell back in disorder.

A close-up of the Richmond Armory carbine showing the lower hump-back lock that began to appear in 1862. (Russ Pritchard collection)

The only true large cavalry battle of the war was Brandy Station in 1863, when Union cavalry attacked Confederate cavalry that were not expecting them. The battle lasted hours and was a see-saw affair, with units dashing about and sabers slashing. It was, however, such a rare event that almost everyone who saw it remarked upon it.

Rosser recalled bringing his brigade forward as a Federal cavalry brigade approached. "When we got to within a hundred yards of each other the Federals halted and my men did the same. Each seemed to dread a collision. The Federal officers rode in front of their men and vainly called on their men to follow, and my efforts and those of my officers to urge my men on were also fruitless," he wrote. "I rode towards the enemy and begged my men to charge, but all this was of no avail." Finally, a Confederate private grabbed his regimental color and charged, and this was the impetus needed to get the others moving. The mounted charge broke the Federal ranks, and the private received a major's commission for his valor.

Such horseback fights were fierce affairs. Rosser was present at Five Forks for mounted fighting there:

While I looked on I saw Major James Breathed, of the horse artillery, attack two Federal captains, Breathed with pistol, and the Federals with sabers. They closed before Breathed had an opportunity to shoot, or if he shot he missed his mark, and when I saw him the Federals were cutting and striking at him with their sabers while Breathed was exceedingly busy warding them off with his pistol. Their horses were run against Breathed's and he was finally knocked off his horse and one of the Federal captains, pulling off one of his boots. Breathed then shot and killed one of the officers and Courier Scruggs dashed out from my side and killed the other. In a moment Breathed was back in the saddle again, with only one boot, and again joined the fight.

Virginia cavalryman John Blue recalled a sharp fight in the Valley of Virginia when the two sides collided:

The Yankees were bearing down on us not fifty yards away at a fast trot, firing their revolvers as they came, a few men and a few horses were struck. Most of their shots were passing over our heads. Then arose that terrible Rebel yell and with drawn saber at a tierce point and rowells buried deep in our horses flanks, at them we went at full speed, when we met the blue and the gray was considerably mixed for a few moments. At the onset we had them at a disadvantage, they having charged with the revolver, whilst we used our saber, their revolvers were now nearly all empty and for a few seconds they were almost defenseless, until they could replace the revolver and draw the saber. This was our

North Carolina cavalry sergeant, 1861

A

Virginia cavalry private, 1864

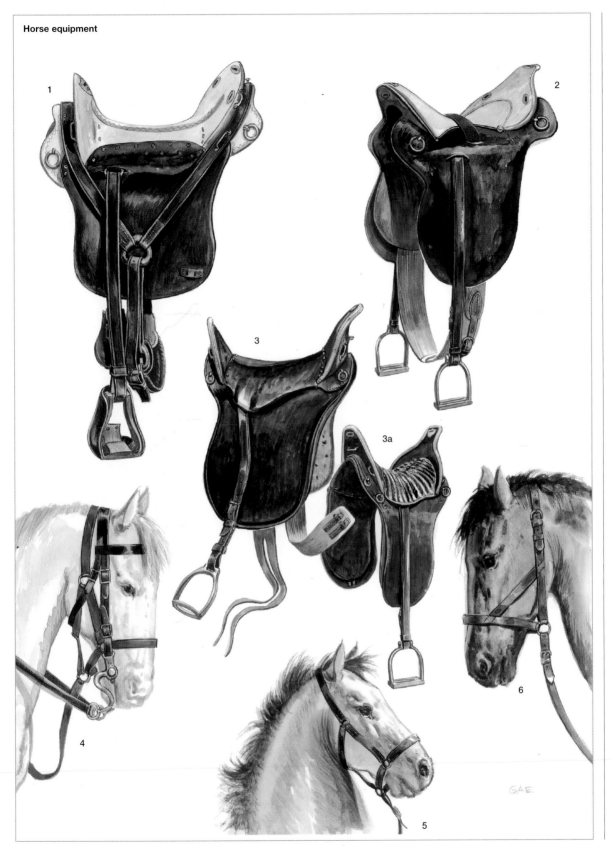

Regimental punishment

D

Raiding a wagon train

E

The cavalry battle

F

A campaign bivouac, mid-winter

G

A hospital scene

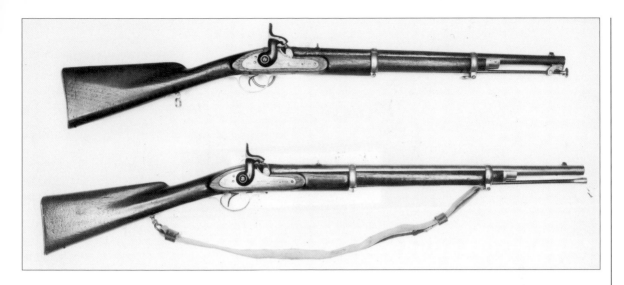

opportunity and we made use of it for a few moments. But it soon became evident the weight of numbers was forcing us back.

Blue and his fellows were forced to retreat or surrender.

The average cavalryman's fight was quite different, however, to those described above. If cavalry went in mounted they simply charged up to the enemy, fired their shotguns, carbines, or revolvers, wheeled about and fell back. Mostly, however, they dismounted and advanced on foot, using their carbines as short muskets.

According to the Laurel Brigade's William McDonald, when his brigade came under command of Wade Hampton, fighting from horseback just about ended. "It was Hampton's favorite method," he wrote:

> to use cavalry as mounted infantry and carbineers, wherever the nature of the country, such as that of the Wilderness, made it practicable; the horses being of use primarily for quickness of movement from one point to another, the fighting being done on foot with carbines. By adopting this use of cavalry, Hampton had by several decades anticipated the universal modern use of mounted soldiers. The introduction of the long-range repeating carbine having rendered the cavalry charge with the saber and pistol almost entire impracticable and obsolete.
>
> The cavalrymen realizing the usual success of Hampton's method, especially where there was to be long-maintained opposition to the enemy's infantry, were willing to dismount and had accepted the use of carbines, which many of them had heretofore despised, preferring to dash in upon the enemy with saber and pistol.

Indeed, the 2nd Virginia's Rev. McKim recalled one saber fight in September 1864 which he called "a rather rare occurrence, for the cavalry were being rapidly transformed into mounted infantry and use the carbine and the repeating rifle much more than the sword."

Hopkins of the 6th Virginia, noted that:

A copy of the British Army's Enfield carbine became the standard Confederate Army design. The Confederate government's own works produced its copies too late to see field use, but private makers in the South started producing these weapons early in the war. (Russ Pritchard collection)

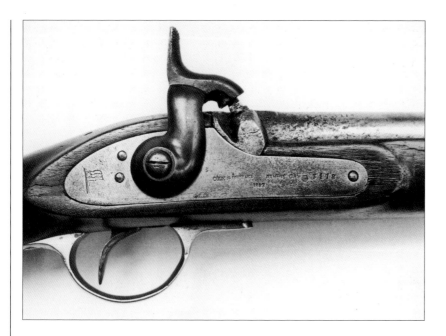

[in action] the cavalry dismounted and fought on foot. This was often done, as the men can do better execution when on the ground, and, besides, they are better protected from the fire of the enemy. On foot, you have to protect you the trees and the rocks and the fences, every little hillock; in fact, anything else that would stop a bullet, but on horseback you are a splendid target for the sharpshooter. Hence, the cavalry on some occasions preferred to be on foot. But when there was any rotating to do, like Richard III, they wanted a horse.

On this particular occasion I was among those chosen to lead the horses. In fact, it always fell to the fourth man. He sat on his horse, while the other three men dismounted and went to the front. These were called the led horses, and, of course, they followed in the rear, keeping as much out of danger as possible.

Traditionally, one of the cavalry's main jobs in battle was to follow up a successful infantry attack, riding among the fleeing enemy and sabering them to the ground. Lieutenant-colonel Arthur Fremantle, a Coldstream Guards officer who visited the Confederacy in 1863, spoke of this practice with Confederate officers:

But to my surprise they [the Confederate officers] all spoke of their cavalry as not efficient for that purpose. In fact, Stuart's men, though excellent at making raids, capturing wagons and stores, and cutting off communications, seem to have no idea of charging infantry under any circumstances. Unlike the cavalry with Bragg's army [of Tennessee], they wear swords, but seem to have little idea of using them – they hanker after their carbines and revolvers. They constantly ride with their swords between their left leg and the saddle, which has a very funny appearance; but their horses are generally good, and they ride well.

However, despite their love of their "carbines and revolvers," not every Confederate cavalryman actually exchanged shots with the enemy. The quartermaster and the quartermaster sergeant were in the rear forwarding ammunition to the front. The adjutant aided the unit commander as needed. The commissary officer made sure food was available for the hungry men once the action was finished. The chaplain had no special post, but picked his own. Rev. McKim of the 2nd Virginia later wrote, "As a chaplain on the firing line with the men, I had nothing to do but sit on my horse and be shot at (unarmed, of course), waiting for a call to attend some wounded man." Company cooks, a position that African-Americans were allowed to fill, were in the rear preparing coffee and food for the wounded.

The regimental surgeon and hospital steward were in their aid station, administering wounded soldiers brought to them by members of the regimental Ambulance Corps. The wounded were often far from medical help, and the regimental hospital system, which gave a surgeon and a hospital steward to each regiment to provide immediate help, was put to the test after each cavalry battle. Moreover, saber wounds often became infected after contact with dirty jeans cloth or wool, leading to the loss of a limb at best. From the aid station, the wounded were transported to the rear to larger hospitals. Once the wounded soldier got back into the army's medical system, he stood a better chance of survival, especially by the time he got back to one of the many large hospitals set up in the Confederacy's leading cities such as Richmond and Atlanta.

PARTISAN RANGERS

Confederate cavalry included not only regular line units, whose job it was to serve as any European cavalry force, but also units of partisan rangers. The idea of fighting behind enemy lines came naturally to those who recalled the American Revolution. Governor Thomas O. Moore of Louisiana, after the fall of New Orleans, issued a proclamation on June 18, 1862, that read in part:

> It is not proper for obvious reasons to state here in detail the measures I have taken and the plans devised for the defense of our homes ... Every able-bodied citizen must hold himself in readiness for immediate active service. Brave, vigilant, energetic officers are authorized to raise bands of Partisan Rangers. Let every possible assistance be rendered them in forming, arming, equipping, and mounting their companies and in giving them support and information when in service.

Following up, on April 23, 1862 the army's adjutant and inspector general issued his General Orders No. 30:

> SECTION 1. The Congress of the Confederate States of America do enact, That the President be, and is hereby, authorized to commission such officers as he may deem proper with authority to form bands of partisan rangers, in companies, battalions or regiments, either as infantry or cavalry, the companies, battalions,

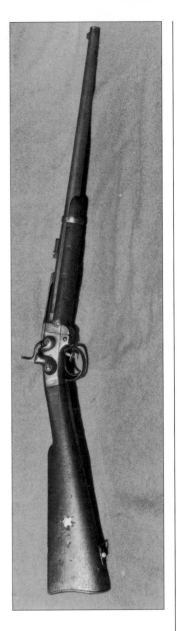

The patented Smith carbine was a US Army weapon that used a rubber cartridge which fitted into a breech that broke open. These cartridges could be refilled and used time and again, so they were useful when captured by Confederate troopers.
(Chris Nelson collection)

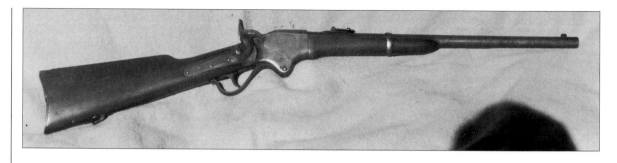

or regiments to be composed each of such numbers as the President may approve.

SEC. 2. Be it further enacted, That such partisan rangers, after being regularly received into service, shall be entitled to the same rations and quarters during their term of service, and be subject to the same regulations as other soldiers.

SEC. 3. Be it further enacted, That for any arms and munitions of war captured from the enemy by any body of partisan rangers and delivered to any quartermaster at such places as may be designated by a commanding general, the rangers shall be paid their full value in such manner as the Secretary of War may prescribe.

Local leaders soon had the chance to raise such partisan companies. John Blue of Western Virginia recalled in 1861 that a local social leader, Isaac Parsons, had returned from a visit to Richmond:

with the authority to raise an independent company of mounted men for border service. This now he under took to do, and in a short time had about 30 men enrolled and organized … Our captain owned a mountain farm known as the Cheshire place, about two miles from Romney, here we first camped, quartermaster and commissary being furnished by our captain. Our arms were principally the home rifle. We had a few flintlock muskets which we found in the loft of the courthouse, also a dozen or so old sabers and perhaps as many horse pistols (flintlocks) all of which had seen service in the Revolution (1775–1783).

A letter dated August 22, 1862 to a John Seawell in Gloucester County, Virginia, is typical of those authorizing local leaders to raise independent companies of mounted men:

Upon the recommendation of Gen. Lee you are authorized to raise one or two companies of partisan rangers (cavalry or infantry) for the defense of Gloucester and the adjacent counties, yourself to be commissioned captain of the first company, and John K. Littleton, of King and Queen, of the second, if it should be organized, from the date of muster into service. These companies must be regularly enlisted for three years or the war, on the same terms as other volunteers, receiving the same bounty, subsistence or commutation, pay, &c., under the same

The US Army's Spencer carbine used metallic cartridges that could not be made in the South, so its use depended on battlefield captures. (Chris Nelson collection)

regulations, and they must be fully organized with the requisite minimum numbers of men, and regularly mustered into the C. S. service. In the absence of a mustering officer you are authorized to muster the companies into service, and you will forward the muster-rolls by the first opportunity to the Adjutant-Gen. The companies must furnish, so far as possible, their own arms and equipments, but your requisitions forwarded to the Chief of Ordnance at Richmond will receive the earliest possible attention, so far as practicable. Being raised within the lines of the enemy and without the scope of the conscription, these companies may receive into their ranks volunteers of any age. Though raised and intended immediately for the defense of their own section of country, yet they are not to be mustered for local service, but will be subject to the orders of the general commanding the military department in which they are included, and to him report must be made when practicable. When communication is impossible you must act on your own responsibility, being the senior captain. All other officers, except the captain in the said company or companies, must be elected.

There was no shortage of men who were only too keen to join a part-time local defense unit, particularly with the added incentive of receiving extra pay for captured enemy equipment. Recruiting was easy. On March 13, 1863, Colonel R. V. Richardson of his "First Tennessee Partisan Rangers" reported that:

Private J.J. Dodd, Co. C, 4th South Carolina Cavalry, holds an M1833 dragoon saber, which probably came from pre-war stocks. (Library of Congress)

On September 6, 1863 [1862], I received authority from the Secretary of War to organize a regiment of Partisan Rangers in Tennessee, subject to your approval or that of Gen. [Sterling] Price. The latter approved, and I immediately came to West Tennessee and began the work. I established a camp and rendezvous in this county, at Galloway's Switch. The enemy at that time held posts at Fort Pillow, Trenton, Humboldt, Jackson, Corinth, Bolivar, and Memphis. The field of my operations for recruiting purposes was necessarily circumscribed by this cordon of military posts, and it has been by fighting and skirmishing with the forces of these places continually that I have been able to hold all of Tipton and Fayette Counties and parts of Haywood, Hardeman, and Shelby Counties. It has required about four months to recruit and organize my regiment.

On February 14, ultimo, I completed the organization by holding an election by ballot for a lieutenant-colonel and major. James U. Green was elected to the first and Berry [B.] Benson to the last named office I also have appointed, subject to the President's

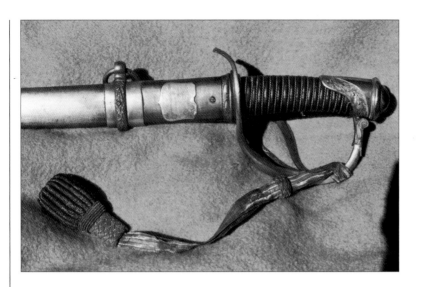

The officer's version of the issue cavalry saber was more heavily engraved than was the enlisted man's. This is a Northern-made M1840 Ames presentation version of the officer's saber. (Chris Nelson collection)

approval, Pinkney M. Pate as quartermaster; Alexander W. Loving, first lieutenant in Capt. R. Burrow's company, as adjutant; George W. Bennett as commissary; Christopher Dickson, M. D., as surgeon; John B. Scarborough, M. D., as assistant surgeon, and Rev. Marion Zelner as chaplain of what I claim to be the First Tennessee Regt. of Partisan Rangers, C. S. Army. I have ten companies organized and five more in process of organization. I had made out full and complete muster-rolls of my companies, but have lost them in a recent engagement with the enemy. I will have them made out again as soon as practicable and forward them. Up to this time I have been acting under orders from Lieut. Gen. [J. C.] Pemberton. I am informed now that you have command of all Confederate forces in Tennessee, and make this hasty report. My efforts to raise a regiment have been attended with much peril and many skirmishes. I have steadily increased, armed, and equipped my force within the enemy's lines. Although cut off from all connections nearly with my Government and superior officers. I have been vested with large discretion, and refer to my general report to Lieut.-Gen. Pemberton as to the manner in which I have exercised it. It will suffice now to say that I had to meet the enemy in overwhelming force the next day after I went into camp in October last, and since that time up to this day some portion or all of my forces have had nearly daily conflicts with him. We have fought two general engagements and have had innumerable skirmishes.

Although Johnston suggested that his unit remained in a permanent camp, partisan rangers operating within Union lines generally had only a handful of men in a regular camp, while most went to various homes to be notified when their services were needed. James Williamson, Co. A, Mosby's Rangers, later wrote,

Having no camps, they made their homes at the farm houses, especially those along the Blue Ridge and Bull Run Mountains. Certain places would be designated at which to meet, but if no time or place had been named at a former meeting, or if necessary to have the command together before a time appointed, couriers were dispatched through the country and the men thus notified.

One danger of men being dispersed when not on duty was that Federal cavalry moved constantly through the same countryside, snapping up individual rangers. Lieutenant John Blue, a member of a western Virginia ranger company, spent one night at his father's house:

> I had been asleep perhaps two hours when I was aroused by the bark of the house dog. After listening a moment, I heard a sound unusual to me. I sprang from the bed and looked from the window. The moon was shining bright almost as day, the ground frozen and covered by a heavy frost. To my horror, I discovered a column of Yankees just entering the yard. I grabbed my clothes and my revolver and rushed downstairs, hoping to make by escape by a back way, but when I opened the door I was met by a Yankee bayonet. I was trapped.

John Mosby, commander of Mosby's Rangers in northern Virginia, wrote, "We lived on the country where we operated and drew nothing from Richmond except the gray jackets my men wore. We were mounted, armed, and equipped entirely off the enemy, but, as we captured a great deal more than we could use, the surplus was sent to supply Lee's army."

While their jackets were gray, much of the rest of their dress came from their Union captures. As Williamson recalled:

> They never masqueraded in the uniforms of Federals, except that through force of circumstances men at time wore blue overcoats captured by them from Federal cavalry. This was done because they could get no others. The Confederate government did not, or could not at all times provide proper clothing, and our soldiers were compelled to wear these to protect themselves from the cold. Rubber blankets were common to both armies and when one was worn it completely hid the uniform.

First South Carolina Sergeant Barry Benson saw Mosby's men and wrote that they:

> were nearly all well dressed, in uniforms each to his own taste, mostly various shades of gray. I noticed that corduroy was much worn, and a handsome uniform it made. Not only were the men better dressed than soldiers ordinarily, but I am quite sure that this band was of better caliber in all respects, physically and mentally, than the general run of soldiers.

Most partisan ranger units were not very well equipped. A typical inspection report of January 1, 1863, reads, "Maj. W. A. Hewlett's battalion Partisan Rangers is stationed at Buttahatche Bridge, 12 miles north of Columbus, on the Aberdeen road. They have 307 double-barrel [shot-] guns and accouterments, 320 sabers and belts, 45 flintlock pistols, 8,320 rounds of cartridges, 4,320 percussion caps; all in good condition."

An M1840 enlisted man's US Army saber. This was the basic saber copied by Southern makers during the war. (*Military Images* magazine)

In contrast to Hewlett's men, Mosby's Rangers, operating in a "target-rich" environment around Washington, DC, were able to capture Union scouts and couriers and quickly armed themselves well. As Mosby recalled, "We used neither carbines nor sabers, but all the men carried a pair of Colt pistols. We did not pay for them but the US Government did." He went on to say:

Stuart's 1st Virginia Cavalry charging the 11th New York Zouaves at the First Manassas. Such assaults with the saber were extremely rare during the war. (*Military Images* magazine)

> My men were as little impressed by a body of cavalry charging them with saber as though they had been armed with cornsticks … I think that my command reached the highest point of efficiency as cavalry because they were well armed with two six-shooters and their charges combined the effect of fire and shock. We were called bushwhackers, as a term of reproach, simply because our attacks were generally surprises and we had to make up by celerity for lack of numbers.

Mosby's men also had two mountain howitzers, which they used with great effect in shelling unguarded wagon trains. Indeed, the command even brought two 12-pounder cannon on at least one raid.

The practice of carrying revolvers was also advantageous because handguns could be kept quiet in holsters, unlike clanking sabers and carbines. As Private Williamson recalled:

> In the stillness of the night the clanking of the sabers and the rattle of the carbines striking against the saddles could be heard for a great distance, and would often betray us when moving cautiously in the vicinity of the Federal camps … The carbine was for long-range shooting. With us the fighting was mostly at close quarters and the revolver was then used with deadly effect.

Beyond simple issues such as uniforms and equipment, the greatest problem associated with the South's partisan rangers was that – as far as both Richmond and generals in the field were concerned – the partisan rangers were too popular. Individuals who would have been more effective for the Confederacy as part of the regular ranks, instead joined local ranger bands. Therefore, on June 13, 1862, army headquarters issued the first of a series of orders limiting partisan ranger recruiting: "Transfers from the line to partisan corps will not be permitted, and if any officer of partisan corps knowingly enlist them from the line, the authority to raise the partisan corps will be revoked, in addition to such punishment as a court-martial may inflict."

On July 31, 1862 it was ordered that, "Persons who are liable to conscription under the act of April 16, 1862, will not be taken to serve as partisan rangers. Such as may be engaged for that branch of service must be over thirty-five years of age." This was followed by an order dated on September 8, 1862 which noted that, "The reception of substitutes into partisan corps is prohibited ..."

One of the major incentives was that partisans shared their loot, unlike regular cavalrymen who had to turn over their captures to headquarters, but more like sailors who got prize money when their ships captured enemy ships. The distribution of the profits of loot was regulated by an order issued on April 21, 1862:

> The act of April 21, 1862, provides that for any arms and munitions of war captured from the enemy by partisan rangers and delivered up at such place as may [be] designated by the commanding general, the rangers shall be paid their full value in such manner as the Secretary of War may prescribe.
>
> The terms "arms and mentions of war" will include all small arms and artillery, ammunition, infantry accouterments, and cavalry equipments, and also cavalry and artillery horses. The animals referred to will be appraised by competent officers, under the orders of the commanding general, and will be paid for when delivered up by any quartermaster, who will take receipt from the parties entitled to receive compensation, and afterward account for the property, as in the case of an ordinary purchase.

"Compensation" paid to rangers for their loot could amount to some serious money. Most rangers, however, said they didn't get rich as a result of their service. Mosby's Rangers were probably the most successful of all partisan ranger bands and Private Williamson recalled with them, "The 'Greenback Raid' was the only one that brought in any great return, and there were only about eighty men who reaped the benefit of it, as the proceeds of a capture went directly to the men

This drawing from life, called a "cavalry charge in Virginia," appeared in *Harper's Weekly* in February 8, 1862. (*Military Images* Magazine)

making it. The acquisition of arms and accoutrements, or even horses, did not make the men wealthy." Of course, any small amount looked impressive to regular Confederate soldiers.

However, although partisan rangers enjoyed the profits of their captures, they were on more shaky ground than regular soldiers when captured. While they were supposed to fight in full Confederate uniform, many wore more of their civilian garb than military dress. This meant that they were often charged as spies. Brigadier-General Daniel Ruggles wrote Union General Benjamin Butler in Louisiana about two such prisoners on July 15, 1862:

> I have received petitions from officers of the First Regt. Louisiana Partisan Rangers touching the case of Henry Castle, jr., a private of Company H, of that regiment, and also an application respecting Thomas C. Pennington, a private of Capt. Wilson Tate's company, of the same regiment, and I deem it expedient to request your early consideration of the subject.
>
> It appears that Private Castle was captured by a detachment of Federal troops in the vicinity of Baton Rouge on or about the 7th of the present month and Private Pennington on or about the 28th day of June; that they were taken to New Orleans, and are held either there or at one of the forts in the vicinity in close confinement, with the threat that they are to be tried and executed as members of a military organization not sanctioned by the laws of civilized warfare. It is to be observed that the first great law of nature, the right of self-defense, is inherent in communities as well as individuals. No law condemns the individual who slays the robber or the assassin, and no just law can condemn a community for using all its power to resist the invader and drive him from their soil …

Ruggles threatened to retaliate by hanging Union prisoners, one for one, if his rangers were hanged.

Fearful of such reprisals, the official policy of the Federal government was, then, to accept the surrender of partisan rangers as prisoners of war. However, this did not prevent the occasional hanging of partisans by Federal troops made angry by ambushes and the deaths of their fellow troops away from the field of, what they considered, fair battle. After one raid, Federals captured and shot three of Mosby's men out of hand, hanging another two, a note pinned to one of them reading, "Such is the fate of all of Mosby's gang."

Confederate cavalry in the streets of Chambersburg, Pennsylvania, during one of their raids on July 30, 1863. The cavalry did not receive the tribute the commander demanded of the town, and so they destroyed some two-thirds of it. (*Frank Leslie's Illustrated News*)

Army headquarters authorized Mosby to kill an equal number of
prisoners in retaliation, and he did so, picking prisoners by lots, leaving
a message with their bodies, "These men have been hung in retaliation
for an equal number of Colonel Mosby's men hung by order of General
Custer at Front Royal. Measure for measure."

At the same time, however, concern was growing about the bad
reputation that Confederate partisan rangers were getting in the
country, both with friends as well as enemies. On July 30, 1862, the
adjutant and inspector general gave orders to Major-General Richard
Taylor, who was about to take over command the District of Western
Louisiana. Taylor was told:

> You will require partisan batteries [companies] organized within
> your command to be carefully inspected, and will disband or
> discharge any that may not give promise of useful service. All
> others you will so direct and control as to make them contribute
> in the greatest degree to the protection of the persons and
> property of our fellow-citizens.

Most generals reported that they had no use for their nearby partisan
rangers. Brigadier-General Daniel Ruggles wrote from Tangipahoa,
Louisiana on July 25, 1862 that, as far as he could see, the "Number of
Partisan Rangers [is] overstated and [they are] without discipline."

Discipline was the most pressing problem for partisan rangers.
General orders issued in the Department of East Tennessee on
September 29, 1862, noted that:

> Information has reached the commanding general that Partisan
> Rangers, cavalry companies, or members thereof, and perhaps
> other connected with the military service, have seized horses, mules,
> wagons, and teams, and other property belonging to alien enemies,
> including East Tennessee who had joined the service of the United

Confederate cavalry attack a Federal supply train near Jasper, Tennessee, in August 1863. Notice the use of carbines rather than sabers; a common practice among western cavalrymen. (*Frank Leslie's Illustrated News*)

States or taken protection under that Government. Such seizures on the part of the military are in conflict with the sequestration laws of the Confederate States and an encroachment upon the jurisdiction of the civil authorities of the land and will not be tolerated. The military therefore are expressly prohibited from seizing or in any manner interfering with property belonging to the calls of persons aforesaid, and all officers and soldiers in this department who have any time taken into their possession any property belonging to alien enemies, including as aforesaid East Tennesseans who have joined the Federal armies or in any manner taken protection under the Government of the United States, are hereby required to report to the receivers at this place the kind and description of property taken, when and from whom, and what disposition has been made of the same, and will at the same time deliver to said sequestration laws of the Confederate States.

North Carolina's governor wrote to Richmond on July 13, 1862:

The large number of partisan rangers authorized, or claimed to be authorized, to be raised by the Department is interfering sadly with the enrollment of conscripts, and would therefore seem to be working a serious injury to the service, unless some great good was to be accomplished by them. I think the teachings of experience show that a long and thorough train age of both men and horses is absolutely required to make cavalry effective, and a rare combination of talent is required for officers to drill or command or use cavalry to advantage. Without these advantages they are useless except for couriers or pickets. They are very expensive and contribute far more than any other corps to exhaust the resources of a country. The idea of being mounted is agreeable to the habits of our people and has attractions which will carry every one into the cavalry that will be allowed to join either cavalry or rangers, to the great detriment of the infantry … Partisan rangers have a kind of separate and independent command, which is another attraction and, I might add, source of detriment. Now, the eagerness of our conscripts to avoid enrollment by enlistment in those independent corps of partisan rangers sadly conflict with the progress of the enrolling officers. The substitutes, particularly, are placed in the rangers. Not believing they will accomplish much good and witnessing the difficulties they throw in the way of enrollment has prompted this communication, and I would suggest that any legal means to check them would be beneficial, particularly should the enrolled conscripts, or their substitutes in particular, be not allowed to go into the partisan rangers. I fear the move may even now be too late.

The Secretary of War wrote to Major-General Samuel Jones, commanding at Knoxville, Tennessee, on October 24, 1862: "The inclosed papers, submitted to the Department by Hon. G. D. Royston, are respectfully referred to you, with the information that much complaint reaches me of the lawlessness of partisan corps within your district and of the oppression practiced by those concerned in the transportation and subsistence of the army."

Major-General Earl Van Dorn wrote from Holly Springs, Mississippi, to the Secretary of War on September 12, 1862: "In regard to Partisan Rangers I respectfully recommend that they be disbanded and that all of conscripts enrolled be turned over to regiments in the field … Isolated companies of Partisan Rangers have no discipline and cannot be depended upon."

Brigadier-General W. N. R. Beall wrote from Port Hudson, Louisiana, on June 8, 1863:

> I have just received your communication containing instructions from the major-general commanding that I shall send 80 men from my line to relieve the Ninth Louisiana Battalion (Partisan Rangers) on Col. Miles' line; that this battalion cannot be trusted on outpost or picket duty; that they are deserting &c., and that I must put them where they can be watched and shot down in case they desert.

Even Colonel Richardson, whose report of great success with his own partisan unit is quoted earlier, ran into trouble because of the actions of

A Virginia civilian rides on the road where Stuart led his first famous raid around the Union Army during the Peninsula Campaign in 1862. (Miller's *Photographic History*)

his men. General Joseph E. Johnston, one of the South's leading generals, wrote Richmond from his headquarters in Chattanooga, Tennessee, on March 6, 1863, "One [R. V.] Richardson, claiming to have authority of the War Department to raise partisan rangers in Mississippi and West Tennessee, is accused of great oppression. If he has any authority, I respectfully recommend that it be withdrawn."

The Confederacy's best partisan unit, Mosby's Rangers, was also not immune from criticism and received Lee's displeasure, with his writing Richmond,

> I greatly commend Maj. Mosby for his boldness and good management. I fear he exercises but little control over his men. He has latterly carried but too few on his expeditions, apparently, and his attention has been more directed toward the capture of wagons than military damage to the enemy. His attention has been called to this.

Speaking of an occasion when his unit stopped a train, Mosby revealed that, "Whether my men got anything in the shape of pocketbooks, watches, or other valuable articles, I never inquired," adding that "I was too busy attending to the destroying of the train to see whether they did."

The reputation of partisan rangers was further damaged by deserters in Confederate uniform, who worked either alone or in small bands to rob civilians while posing as regular Confederate partisan rangers. In Northern Virginia Mosby fought a serious a war against these deserters, but nobody could stop their outrages. The further west one went, the greater the outrages and the more undisciplined the partisan rangers.

A private in the Union's 20th Illinois Infantry in Alabama in 1863 recalled how, "One poor fellow strayed a little from a foraging party; was caught by some bush-wackers, who cut off his ears and nose and otherwise mutilated him, then let him go. His head was badly swollen when he reached us, and he died a few days later."

The most lawless partisan rangers fought a guerrilla war in Missouri and Kansas against Federal soldiers and citizens alike. There, a Southern sympathizer named William Quantrill received a direct commission from Jefferson Davis to organize a partisan ranger company. His company included men who became well-known post-war outlaws in the west, such as Cole Younger and Jesse and Frank James. Similar companies were raised by such men as "Bloody Bill" Anderson. These men did not wear regulation uniform, instead preferring "guerrilla shirts," which were cut low in front and

Crews repair the damage to the Orange & Alexandria Railroad at Catlett's Station on August 22, 1862. The raid by Stuart's cavalry saw Confederate cavalrymen capture 220 horses and all the Union commanding general's personal baggage. (Miller's *Photographic History*)

had four large pockets, usually trimmed with colored tape, and were worn outside the trousers. Many of these shirts were decorated with elaborate needlework, done by mothers or sweethearts. These hardcore partisans were armed with two to eight revolvers and a carbine, making them formidable enemies.

The men in these bands admitted that they had chosen to fight their way, rather than join regular Confederate units, for more than just patriotism. Anderson wrote to a newspaper in Lexington, Missouri, explaining that:

> I have chosen guerrilla warfare to revenge myself for wrongs that I could not honorably avenge otherwise … [The Federals] Revenged themselves by murdering my father, destroying all my property, and have since that time murdered one of my sisters and kept the other two in jail twelve months. But I have fully gutted my vengeance. I have killed many, I am a guerrilla. I have never belonged to the Confederate Army, nor do my men … I have tried to war with the Federals honorably, but for retaliation I have done things, and am fearful will have to do that I would shrink from if possible to avoid." Anderson signed himself, "Commanding Kansas First Guerrillas."

A cavalry skirmish line advances in this illustration by famed artist Edwin Forbes. (*Military Images* magazine)

The highlight of both Anderson's and Quantrill's war was the almost total destruction of Lawrence, Kansas, on August 21, 1863. Quantrill's orders were to "Kill every man big enough to carry a gun," and the defenseless town was quickly overrun, its stores looted, buildings set on fire, and saloons broken into, leading to drunken rangers.

Confederate regular soldiers were appalled by this behavior, and on February 1864, the commander on the scene wrote to the department commander:

> Quantrill will not obey orders and so much mischief is charged to his command here that I have determined to disarm, arrest, and send his entire command to you or General Smith … They regard the life of a man less than you would that of a sheep-killing dog. Quantrill and his men are determined never to go into the army or fight in any general battle, first, because many of them are deserters from our Confederate ranks, and next, because they are afraid of being captured, and then because it won't pay men who fight for plunder.

The Secretary of War asked Lee what he thought about the problem, and on April 3,

1864, Lee replied that:

> Experience has convinced me that it is almost impossible, under the best officers even, to have discipline in these bands of Partisan Rangers, or to prevent them from becoming an injury instead of a benefit to the service, and even where this is accomplished the system gives license to many deserters & marauders, who assume to belong to these authorized companies & commit depredations on friend & foe alike. Another great objection to them is the bad effect upon the discipline of the army from the constant desire of the men to leave their commands & enjoy the great license allowed in these bands. With the single exception mentioned [Mosby's Rangers], I hope the order will be issued at once disbanding the companies & battalions serving in this department.

Confederate officials determined to take steps to correct the problem. One approach was to turn the partisan ranger bands into regular Confederate cavalry units. On December 23, 1862, Richmond notified Colonel J.D. Imboden, then commanding the 1st Virginia Partisan Rangers:

> Under the various orders which from time to time have been given yourself and others relative to the raising and organizing of troops in Western Virginia, much confusion and difficulty have arisen, and with the view of harmonizing these difficulties, and rendering the branch of the service with which you have been connected still more effective, the Secretary of War directs me to invite your co-operation in an endeavor to change your entire present organization from partisan rangers to a regular command for the war. You will be intrusted with the reorganization of the whole force in the section of country in which you are now engaged, and authorized to fill up the old companies and regiments with conscripts, and to recruit all the men you can from counties within the enemy's lines and also from non-conscripts. From the energy and zeal you have displayed in the service, the Department has no hesitation in committing to you this important undertaking, and it is hoped, in view of the public interests, that you will at once signify your willingness to make the desired change and engage in the new duties proposed. Should you do this, all former orders for the organization of troops in the disputed country will be withdrawn. Of course, it is understood that the consent of the men now enrolled as partisan rangers must be obtained before the desired change can be undertaken, and this consent it will be necessary for you to secure as a preliminary step in the matter.

The problem was that too many partisan rangers saw no reason to give up the nice jobs they had to become cavalrymen, who would be under strict army discipline and might be forced to leave their home areas. Most declined the change. Therefore, on June 12, 1863, the army's adjutant and inspector general acted:

> The second section of the act entitled and act to organize partisan rangers provides that such partisan rangers, after being regularly

Colonel John S. Mosby poses with a saber, a weapon he discarded early in the war, in this engraving made from a period photograph. Mosby rejected the saber in favor of the pistol he wears in his holster.

received into service, shall be entitled to the same pay, rations, and quarters during their term of service and be subjected to the same regulations as other soldiers. The irregularities reported to this Department as having been committed by such corps renders it proper that these corps shall be placed under stricter regulations than those heretofore adopted. The generals commanding the department in which they are serving are hereby authorized to combine them into battalions and regiments with the view to bringing them under the same regulations movements; and the same officers will recommend any further measures for their organization as an integral portion of their commands as will in their opinion promote their efficiency and the interest of the service. The general of the department will recommend field officers for the organizations that may be made, to be submitted for the consideration of the President. Such partisan corps as are serving within the enemy's lines are for the present excepted from this order.

It was still not enough. The rangers remained out of control and complaints about their behavior persisted. Finally, on February 17, 1864, Congress passed this bill:

The Congress of the Confederate States of America do enact, That the act of Congress aforesaid be, and the same is hereby, repealed: Provided, That organizations of partisan rangers acting as regular cavalry at the passage of this act, shall be continued in their present organization: Provided, They shall hereafter be considered as regular cavalry and not as partisan rangers.

SEC. 2. That all the bands of partisan rangers organized under the said act, may, as the interests of the service allow, be united with other organizations, or be organized into battalions and regiments, with the view to bringing them under the general conditions of the Provisional Army as to discipline, control and movements, under such regulations as the Secretary of War may prescribe.

SEC. 3. The Secretary of War shall be authorized, if he deems proper, for a time, or permanently, to except from the operation of this act such companies as are serving within the lines of the enemy, and under such conditions as he may prescribe.

A drawing of Union cavalry recapturing a wagon train that had just been taken by Mosby's Rangers from *Frank Leslie's Illustrated News.*

Under this final section, units like Mosby's Rangers, operating behind Union lines in Northern Virginia, were still officially sanctioned. Indeed, Mosby's Rangers did not disband until after Lee's surrender of the Army of Northern Virginia, on April 21, 1865. Out west, however, it was not until Anderson was killed in a running gun fight on October 26, 1864, and Quantrill was mortally wounded when his camped company was surprised on May 10, 1865, that the bloody rides of Confederate partisan rangers ended.

SCOUTS AND COURIERS

The third and fourth types of cavalry mentioned by visiting German officer, Captain Justus Scheibert, in 1863 were scouts and couriers. Staff officer John Esten Cooke later wrote about the army's scouts:

The scout proper is "commanding in the field," with no one near to give him orders. He goes and comes at will, having that about him which all pickets obey. He is "on detached service," and having procured certain information, reports to the officer who has sent him, without intermediate ceremony. Operating within the enemy's lines at all times, he depends for success and safety on the quickness of his eye and hand – and his reliance on these is great. He is silent in his movements, low-toned in his speech, abstemious in his habits, and as untiring on the track of the enemy as the Cuban blood-hound on the trail of the fugitive. He sleeps rarely in houses, preferring the woods; and always slumbers "with one eye open," on the look out for his enemy.

The scout has a thorough knowledge of the country, and is even acquainted with "every hog path." He travels in the woods; and often in crossing a sandy highway dismounts, and backs his horse across the road, to mislead the enemy, on the watch of "guerrillas," as to the direction of his march. He thus "flanks" their pickets, penetrates to their camps, reconnoitres their number and position, and strives to pick up some straggler whom he can pump for information. Thus lurking and prowling around the enemy's camps, by night and day, the scout never relaxes his exertions until he discovers what he wishes. That discovery once made – of the strength, situation, and probably designs of the enemy – the stealthy emissary "snakes" back as he came; mounts his trusty steed in the depth of the wood; and first listening attentively, sets out on his return with his supply of valuable information.

Out west, John N. Porter joined the 1st Kentucky Cavalry in November 1861. According to him, "The object of the organization was to furnish guides and scouts for the Army." The 1st Kentucky did not generally engage in pitched battles or major raids, as did regular cavalry outfits. Porter described his normal duty:

Many a night have I been roused from sleep in my tent, with orders to report to Headquarters for instructions. I would receive the necessary orders, the countersign would be whispered in my ear, and the next moment the sentinel at the door would pass me out, and three or four of us would mount upon fleet and spirited horses.

A few miles out of town we would be stopped by pickets. Giving the countersign, we were then out alone in the darkness and our own

Mosby, standing, center, holding his hat, with some Maryland members of his partisan ranger battalion. Note the near regulation Confederate uniforms, which they could get made at home from superior material to that used for issue uniforms. (Library of Congress)

thoughts. How can I or anyone describe the thoughts we had except we were serving the cause? We would remain silent for long periods. Our destination was often Morgantown, Woodbury, and Rochester, and though attended with no great open danger, it was not devoid of peril...

Now and then we would call and see our friends at home, eat at a table, and use a knife and fork.

The assistance rendered to the Army by means of these Scouts was very great.

In every direction, toward the enemy, these scouts were continually away on outposts, many times within enemy lines. Many sharp skirmishes among the first fighting in the State [of Kentucky] were in giving help to the Cavalry in piloting detachments to the enemy's position.

In other cases men did not join a unit specifically labeled as "scouts," but rather a regular cavalry unit that was assigned this duty. As with partisan rangers, men on scouting duty, in either a specially recruited unit or a regular unit assigned the duty, were authorized to keep the money they made from captures of any Federal equipment. For example, John Gill, then in the 1st Maryland Cavalry Battalion, was a member of a small party of scouts that captured some 23 horses and seven prisoners.

A few days later Captain Blackford came into camp and handed me six hundred dollars in gold as my share of the proceeds of the sale of the horses. This was a privilege accorded to scouts and not to regular army officers and privates. I always sent this to my banker in Richmond, to be applied equally for credit of my brother and myself, the former being in the infantry. This gave us plenty of money for some months to come, and enabled us to keep up a respectable outfit.

Mosby, seated center with the hat with the feather in the brim. Alongside Mosby are more of his men, this time mostly in Confederate central government issued jackets. (Miller's *Photographic History*)

Some scouting expeditions were behind enemy lines. Porter recalled one such mission where the scouts disguised themselves: "Our dress consisted of a Federal uniform over the Confederate one." If captured in such dress, however, the scouts were liable to be quickly strung up as spies.

Scouts and couriers were often armed more lightly than regular cavalry. I.N. Rainey, Co. A, 7th Tennessee Cavalry, which was dedicated to courier service, recalled that, "Formerly we were armed with Carbine Pistol and saber, later, with only Pistol and saber. Our principal duties were courier riding and dispatch carrying," he wrote. "Often on the Battlefield we had to deliver orders from our General to officers on the most dangerous part of the field. Sometimes on a duty, the performance of which took long rides of several days."

SELECT BIBLIOGRAPHY

Albaugh, William, *Confederate Edged Weapons*, Harper & Brothers, New York, 1960

Albaugh, William, Hugh Benet Jr., Edward Simmons, *Confederate Handguns*, Broadfoot Publishing, Wilmington, North Carolina, 1993

Blackford, Susan Leigh, *Letters from Lee's Army*, A.S. Barnes & Co., New York, 1947

Brown, Norman, *One of Cleburne's Command*, University of Texas Press, Austin, Texas, 1980

Crabb, Martha L., *All Afire to Fight*, Avon Books, New York, 2000

Hale, Douglas, *The Third Texas Cavalry in the Civil War*, University of Oklahoma Press, Norman, Oklahoma, 1993

Hopkins, Luther, *From Bull Run To Appomattox*, Fleet-McGinley, Baltimore, Maryland, 1908

Lord, Francis, editor, *The Fremantle Diary*, Little, Brown & Co., Boston, 1954

McDonald, William N., *A History of the Laurel Brigade*, Olde Soldier Books, Gaithersburg, Maryland, 1987

McGowan, Stanley S., *Horse Sweat and Powder Smoke*, Texas A&M University Press, College Station, Texas, 1999

Mosby, John S., *The Memoirs of*, Indiana University Press, Bloomington, Indiana, 1959

Oates, Dan, *Hanging Rock Rebel*, Burd Street Press, Shippensburg, Pennsylvania, 1994

Ross, Fitzgerald, *Cities and Camps of the Confederate States*, University of Illinois Press, Urbana, Illinois, 1958

Scott, Robert N., editor, *The War of the Rebellion: A Compilation of the Official Records of the Union and Confederate Armies*, Washington, D.C., 1880

Summers, Festus, P., *Borderland Confederate*, University of Pittsburg Press, Pittsburg, Pennsylvania, 1962

Trout, Robert J., *Riding with Stuart*, White Mane, Shippensburg, Pennsylvania, 1994

Williamson, James J., *Mosby's Rangers*, Ralph B. Kenyon, New York, 1896

John Hunt Morgan's cavalry is shown raiding a western town in this engraving that appeared in the New York publication, *Harper's Weekly*.

Cavalry scouts photographed near Gettysburg, Pennsylvania, in 1863. (Miller's *Photographic History*)

GLOSSARY

Camp of instruction Training location for new recruits.

Cantle Rear portion of a saddle.

Cantonment areas Temporary lodging or military station; a camp ground.

Carbines A short rifle favored by cavalry.

Company Q Unofficial name given to a company within some Confederate regiment, that was staffed by men who were unfit for duty. Usually comprised of the lazy, the cowardly, and the wounded.

Countersign The required reply to a challenge from a sentry.

Fuller A groove or ridge in the blade of a sword or other weapon.

Halter A cord or strap used for leading a horse.

Haversack Canvas bag worn either from shoulder to hip or attached to the saddle.

Jeans cloth   Cotton and wool mixture fabric frequently used in the manufacture of Confederate uniforms.

Kepi A French style military cap with a flat circular top and a horizontal peak.

Knapsack Canvas bag that was worn on the soldier's back.

Militia A military force raised from the civilian population in order to supplement regular forces. Militia were comprised of men who were legally liable to military service, without enlistment.

Neatsfoot oil   A light oil obtained from the feet and shinbones of cattle that was occasionally used to dress horses wounds.

Partisan rangers Units raised to serve behind enemy lines.

Persimmon lightening A homemade alcohol drink.

Pickets Troops sent out to watch for the enemy.

Quart Measure of capacity equivalent to two pints.

Raiding A campaign made into territory without a plan to permanently retain or garrison the land afterwards.

Rebel Yell Characteristic battle cry used by the Confederates throughout the Civil War.

Richmond The capital city of Virginia, located on the James River. It was the capital of the Confederacy during the Civil War.

Rowells A small spiked revolving wheel or disk at the end of a spur.

Skirmish A small battle.

Sutlers Individuals authorized to sell small items, for example, food, boot polish, sewing and writing equipment, to a specific regiment.

Tierce point A recognized parrying position in fencing. The sword-hand is in pronation, protecting the upper portion of the body.

Valise Small piece of luggage hung from a saddle.

Yankees Person from New England or the northern states of the US.

COLOR PLATE COMMENTARY

PLATE A: NORTH CAROLINA CAVALRY SERGEANT, 1861

North Carolina provided its men with uniforms that were made within the state, and which conformed to state regulations (1). The branch of service color for cavalry was yellow, and it was worn on the epaulet, chevrons, and as a stripe down each trouser leg. Our cavalryman wears a white buff leather M1840 dragoon saber belt with a brass oval belt plate bearing the block-letters 'NC' (also 3).On the right front hip he wears a cap pouch (also 4). Hanging from the belt is an M1860 US cavalry saber with brass hilt a US Army version of the French M1822 cavalry saber (also 2), leather grip wrapped with brass wire, and a shiny iron scabbard (also 2a). He also holds a Colt Carbine rifle as was supplied with pre-war state munitions, not the more typically issued Colt Rifle (9,9a – see below).

The white buff leather sword belt is of pre-war manufacture, with a Northern-made state belt plate worn with it. Also shown are two of the knives typically carried by early-war volunteers, a "D-guard" Bowie knife (8) and a straight-bladed "Arkansas toothpick" (7). The tin drum canteen is typical of what was made in the South, especially early in the war, as is the plain canvas haversack in which the soldier's rations were carried.

9 and 9a (detail) are an M1855 Colt percussion revolving rifle, made on essentially the same design as the Colt revolver, with six shots for each load. The weapon was not a great success, as there was usually a gas leak between the cylinder and the barrel at each shot, and this could set off the other unfired rounds in the cylinder. One had to be careful not to rest the weapon's forend on one's hand, or the hand could well be lost as a result.

A modern reconstruction of a typical Confederate cavalryman. The jacket and trousers are made of logwood-dyed jeans cloth. The carbine is a Smith breechloader, while the revolver in the holster is a 0.36-caliber Colt "Navy." Note how the jacket is worn buttoned only at the throat, a popular way of wearing the jacket that conformed to regulations, while still allowing air to reach the body. The flag is a copy of those carried in Hardee's Corps of the Army of Tennessee, one of which was carried by the 17th/18th Texas Cavalry Regiment (Dismounted). (*Military Images* magazine)

Also featured on this plate are a commonly issued canteen (5) and ration bag (6).

PLATE B: VIRGINIA CAVALRY PRIVATE, 1864

A fully equipped cavalryman (1), as this private is, would carry a carbine attached to a sling with an iron hook (7). In this case, the carbine is a Southern-made J.P. Murray muzzle-loading carbine. The fact that most Confederates were used to muzzle-loading carbines, while the Federals habitually used breech-loading carbines put the Confederates at a real disadvantage in action since reloading a muzzle loader was slower and harder.

The private has an M1860 Colt "Army" revolver (2) and an M1860 light cavalry saber (5), both captured from the enemy. His otherwise plain uniform is trimmed in yellow, something many cavalrymen tried to do for themselves. Trim sent from home was later applied to the all-gray issued uniform.

Also seen on this plate are spurs (8), cartridge box (4), sling belt (6), and belt buckle (3).

PLATE C: HORSE EQUIPMENT

1: The M1859 US saddle, better known as the "McClellan saddle." The saddle takes its name from its designer; US Army Major General George B McClellan, who based it on a Hungarian model he saw during his tour of Europe as a military observer.

2: The 1860 patent Jenifer saddle, which was adopted as the official saddle of the Confederate Army. This saddle came with a curved valise that fitted to the cantle and had an opening in its center, through which the user could put and take items. According to the Confederate chief of ordnance, the Jenifer saddle "did very well while the horses were in good condition … but it came down on the horse's backbone and withers as soon as the cushion of fat and muscle dwindled." The saddle was then dropped in favor of the McClellan saddle, which sat more comfortably on a horse's back.

3: The Grimsley saddle, as modified and manufactured in the South for the Confederate cavalry. This saddle had been adopted by the US Army in 1847 for its dragoons and saw use until the McClellan saddle replaced it in 1859. However, a number of officers continued to use the Grimsley saddle, which they had become accustomed to over the years, throughout the war although they slightly adapted it (3a).

4: A bridle commonly used at this time.

5: A Confederate ordnance-department-made halter that uses rings instead of halter squares and bolts, which were beyond Southern manufacturing capacity. This halter was used through February 1863, when its production was limited to sales to officers.

6: This simple style of halter became the most common

Confederate issue halter after February 1863. It was described as " … one + a quarter inch wide with two buckles + one ring, head + nose peace [sic] passing through it, no front peace [sic], no throat band and stitched eight stitches to the inch and made of good southern tanned leather …"

PLATE D: REGIMENTAL PUNISHMENT

One cavalryman has been made to "ride" a wooden horse with a giant wooden sword, something to embarrass a soldier whose performance was less than stellar. Nearby, another soldier, being punished for intoxication, is made to stand for hours on end with a wooden log held over one shoulder. A third soldier is being bucked and gagged, with a piece of wood placed through the mouth and tied behind the head, while his hands are tied in front with his arms under a stick of wood that passes beneath his knees. Such punishment would weaken a man to the point that he would be unable to stand for hours after his release.

PLATE E: RAIDING A WAGON TRAIN

The high point for a cavalryman's campaign, be he a regular cavalryman, scout, or partisan ranger, was capturing a wagon train. However, the men were often so involved in obtaining plunder, ranging from new clothes to liquor, that they frequently let the wagon get away safely. Most regular cavalry units would try to return the captured train to the main army, while scouts and partisan rangers would simply burn the wagons after they were looted.

PLATE F: THE CAVALRY BATTLE

While true mounted cavalry battles were rare, they did happen from time to time. When they did they were simply mounted brawls, with little command and control as the men broke ranks to mix it up with the Federals.

PLATE G: A CAMPAIGN BIVOUAC, MID-WINTER

Camped on the scene of what had clearly been a skirmish the night before – judging from the dead Federal cavalryman in the distance – some cavalrymen try to sleep wrapped in their blankets while others in the early dawn hours have risen. Two officers in the distance, wrapped in their blankets to keep out the cold, look towards enemy lines, where a home has gone up in flames, undoubtedly burned by Federal raiders.

PLATE H: A HOSPITAL SCENE

A volunteer writes a letter for a badly wounded cavalryman, while a surgeon, indicated by the black collar and cuffs and green sash, overlooks his patients in this formal hospital. The Chrimbozo Hospital in Richmond was the largest hospital in North America by the war's end. The Chrimbozo even had its own herd of dairy cattle.

INDEX